Here's all the great literature in this grade level of *Celebrate Reading!*

MARTIN LUTHER KING, JR.

I HAVE A DREAM

WRITINGS AND SPEECHES THAT CHANGED THE WORLD

Anne Frank
The Diary of a Young Girl

FOREWORD BY CORETTA SCOTT KING

Hatchet
GARY PAULSEN

ROOTS
The Saga of an American Family
ALEX HALEY

Mirror, Mirror
And Other Reflections

Featured Poets
T. S. Eliot
Lillian Morrison
Margaret Danner

Book A Celebrate Reading!

Triumph of the Human Spirit
Meeting Challenges

Hatchet
GARY PAULSEN

BC 60609-4/$4.99 U.S./$6.50 CAN. CLASSIC/POCKET BOOKS

Out of the millions who were silenced forever, one
voice remains to remind us—the voice of
Anne Frank
The Diary
of a Young Girl

Without a Map

Searching for Who You Are

Book C Celebrate Reading!

You Have Seen Our Faces

Stories About America

A NOVEL OF SACAGAWEA
by award-winning author
SCOTT O'DELL
Streams to
the River,
River to the Sea
A brave
Indian princess
finds adventure
and love...

FAWCETT JUNIPER

CROW and WEASEL
by Barry Lopez
Illustrations by Tom Pohrt

More Great Books to Read!

Queen of Hearts
by Vera and Bill Cleaver

Julie of the Wolves
by Jean Craighead George

After the Dancing Days
by Margaret Rostkowski

Prairie Songs
by Pam Conrad

Jacob Have I Loved
by Katerine Paterson

The Upstairs Room
by Johanna Reiss

The Mouse Rap
by Walter Dean Myers

Shark Beneath the Reef
by Jean Craighead George

You Have Seen Our Faces

STORIES ABOUT AMERICA

The Cover Story

John Van Hammersveld did the collage for the front and back covers. He has also done an album cover for the Rolling Stones, a wall mural for the Olympics near the Coliseum in Los Angeles, the design for a surfing magazine, and many well-known posters.

ISBN: 0-673-80085-7

Acknowledgments appear on page 144.

45678910RRS99989796959493

You Have Seen Our Faces

STORIES ABOUT AMERICA

ScottForesman

A Division of HarperCollins*Publishers*

Contents

VOICES

VISIONS

STUDENT RESOURCES

Meeting Uncle Jed

BY CAROLYN REEDER

Will sighed and tipped his hat so the brim shaded his eyes from the late afternoon sun. Now, if only he could block out the monotonous creaking of the buggy wheels.

Doc Martin pointed to a small cluster of buildings on the right and said, "Shouldn't be much farther now. They live just a couple of miles beyond the store and the mill."

Will looked at the motionless waterwheel and frowned. The mill wasn't grinding, so food must be as scarce in the Virginia Piedmont as it was in the Shenandoah Valley. Another reason his aunt's family would probably be as sorry to see him as he would be to see them. He scrunched lower in his seat.

The doctor took a handkerchief from his pocket and mopped his florid face.

"I know how you feel about coming here, Will," he said, "but it's what your mother wanted. Her instructions were quite clear—if anything happened to her and your father, you children were to go to her sister."

A t the mention of his family, Will felt the familiar burning behind his eyes. He clenched his jaw and waited until he could speak without his voice trembling. Then he said stiffly, "She wrote out those instructions a long time ago. That letter you showed me was dated before the war. She'd never have wanted us—wanted me—to live with traitors."

Doc Martin sighed heavily. "We've been through all this before, Will. You know this is the way it has to be, so you might as well make the best of it."

Will gritted his teeth. He hated to be preached at. And there was more to come.

"I don't want to hear any more about traitors, either. Your uncle wasn't a traitor. He didn't help the Yankees, he just didn't fight them. I don't approve of that any more than you do, Will, but the war's over. It's time to forget the bitterness."

Forget? Will swallowed hard. It was fine for Doc Martin to talk. The war hadn't ruined *his* life. *His* father and brother hadn't been killed by the Yankees. *His* little sisters hadn't died in one of the epidemics that had spread from the encampments into the city. And *his* mother hadn't turned her face to the wall and slowly died of her grief.

Will pushed back his hat and glared at Doc Martin. "You don't have as much to feel bitter about as I do," he said.

Doc Martin's gray eyes looked sad behind his spectacles. "You don't think four years of seeing young men die is enough to make a doctor bitter?"

Will's anger drained away. "I—I'm sorry, Doc. I guess I wasn't thinking," he muttered. They rode on in silence, and Will felt an empty sadness. This might be the last time he'd ever see Doc Martin. Why had he spoiled their time together?

Finally he asked, "Shouldn't we be there by now? It seems like we've gone at least two miles since the mill."

"We should be getting there," agreed Doc Martin. Reining in the horse, he brought the buggy to a stop beside a girl who was walking along the edge of the road, gathering something into a basket. "Could you tell me if Jed and Ella Jones live near here, miss?"

The girl looked up, her blue eyes wide. Brushing a loose strand of light brown hair off her face with one hand, she nodded, staring from Doc Martin to Will and then letting her eyes linger on Chauncy, the stout Morgan that pulled the buggy. "It's on the left a little way beyond the creek," she said finally, pointing down the road.

Will glanced down at the girl. She looked about ten, two years younger than he. He caught his breath and took a closer look, thinking how much she resembled his sister Betsy. Their eyes met, and Will looked away, embarrassed that the barefoot country girl with a smudge of dirt on her cheek had caught him staring.

"Thank you, miss," said Doc Martin, clucking to his horse.

At the shallow creek, the horse stopped to drink, and Will looked back. The girl was standing in the road, watching them.

They forded the stream easily and turned in at the grassy lane that left the road by a large chestnut tree. Will looked ahead at the house that would be his new home. It was a small house built of squared logs, with a porch across the front and a stone chimney at one end. Nearby stood a still smaller building—he guessed it was the summer kitchen. There was a henhouse with an empty yard, a small barn that obviously had been unoccupied for some time, and several other small, weathered buildings.

Beyond the house he could see a garden patch enclosed by a stone fence, but the fields on both sides of the lane lay fallow. As they neared the house, a woman came out onto the porch.

Will had never met his Aunt Ella, but he knew her at once. Her clothes were worn and faded and her hair was graying, but the way she stood and the proud way she held her head reminded him so much of his mother that his chest ached.

Doc Martin stopped the buggy, lowered his bulky frame to the ground, and tied the reins to the pasture fence. Will scrambled down and stood uncertainly for a moment, then followed Doc toward the house.

Doc Martin stopped at the foot of the porch steps and doffed his hat. "Mrs. Jones?" he said. "I'm Dr. George Martin. I tended your sister in her last illness and I've brought you her boy, Will."

Aunt Ella drew a quick breath and then hurried down the steps to welcome Will. Suddenly he was confused. Part of him wanted to run to her and be held close, but part of him wanted to back away. Taking a deep breath, he stepped forward and grasped her outstretched hands in his. "Hello, Aunt Ella," he said, trying to keep his voice steady.

Tears welled up in her eyes as she squeezed his hands and said, "I never even knew she was ill. . . . But what about Betsy and Eleanor? Didn't they come, too?"

"I'll unhitch Chauncy and put him in the pasture," Will said, pulling away and leaving Doc Martin to explain how the little girls had died of typhoid last summer. And to tell what had happened to Charlie. The pulse began to pound in his temples the way it always did when Will thought of his brother's senseless death at the hands of the Yankees.

Methodically, Will led Chauncy into the pasture. He

knew it was foolish to unhitch the horse when Doc Martin would be leaving soon, but he'd needed to escape. He was replacing the rails in the pasture gate when a voice at his elbow said, "I'll get him a bucket of water."

He turned and saw the girl they'd met on the road, with her basketful of some kind of wild greens. In a flash he realized why she had reminded him of his sister Betsy—she was his cousin Meg!

"He had a drink at the creek," Will said.

"He might want more," the girl said, eyeing the horse wistfully. "The army got our Nell," she added.

Will looked up in surprise. "Did the Yankees come through here?" he asked.

"The Yankees came through, all right. But it was the rebels that got Nell. They took everybody's horses for the cavalry."

Farm horses like Nell probably ended up pulling artillery guns, Will thought as he watched the girl hurry to the barn and come back carrying a wooden bucket. He waited for her to notice that it was full of spiderwebs and shriek and drop it, but she simply wiped it out with a handful of tall grass and headed off toward the spring.

On the porch, Doc Martin and Aunt Ella were still deep in conversation. Will guessed they must be talking about his mother's long illness. He leaned against the fence and watched Chauncy flicking the flies with his tail as he grazed. Will scowled, wishing his cousin hadn't called the Confederates "rebels." How that word grated on his ears! Then he heard soft footsteps behind him and turned to see Meg struggling with the heavy water bucket.

"Here, I'll carry that," he said, hurrying toward her.

"No, I'll take it to him."

Will shrugged and watched her gently pat the horse's flank.

"I really miss our Nell," she said.

"At least the Yankees didn't get her, Meg."

The girl's eyes narrowed and she asked, "How did you know my name?"

He looked away. "I figured it out," he said stiffly. "I'm your cousin Will, from Winchester."

"When I saw you and your pa on the road I wondered who you were!"

"That's not my father," Will said flatly. "My father was killed in the war."

Meg's hands flew to her face. "Oh, I'm sorry!" she said. And then, curiosity getting the better of her, she asked, "But then who is that man you're with?"

"That's Doc Martin. He brought me here." Will kicked at a rock buried in the grass.

Meg stared at him for a moment. "Then your ma must be dead, too," she said slowly, "and he's brought you here to stay."

Still kicking at the rock, Will nodded.

"But what about your sisters? Are they—"

Quickly, he nodded again. "And so's Charlie, my brother. Killed by the Yankees two years ago."

"So you're all that's left of your family."

Will turned away. "Doc's about ready to leave," he said, reaching for Chauncy's halter. He led the horse out of the pasture and hitched him to the buggy. Just as he finished unloading his belongings, Doc Martin came and stood beside him.

"I wish things could be different," Doc said, resting his hand on Will's shoulder. "There's nothing I'd like better than to have you with me in Winchester. But even if your mother hadn't left that letter, it wouldn't have worked out. A bachelor doctor who's out on calls at all hours and away half the night on confinements can't provide the kind of home a boy needs."

Will gave a jerky nod. "I understand, sir."

"These are good people, Will," Doc Martin went on. "Poor, but good. And they're kin. You'll do fine here— it's a lot different from what you're used to, but you'll do fine."

"I know I will, sir," Will said, hoping he sounded more confident than he felt.

Doc Martin climbed awkwardly into the buggy and then looked down at the thin, dark-haired boy. "Goodbye, Will," he said. His left eye began to twitch, just as it had the night he'd come into Will's room to tell him of his mother's death, and without waiting for a reply he urged Chauncy forward.

As the buggy began to roll down the lane, a feeling of desolation almost overcame Will. Aunt Ella laid her hand on his arm, and her touch calmed him a little.

"Let's move your things inside," she said, turning him away from the sight of the disappearing buggy. "You'll have the room where Sam and Enos used to sleep," she

continued. "The twins have gone to Ohio to find work—
they'll be sending us their pay to help out."

Will barely listened. He was concentrating on regain-
ing his self-control. But when his aunt stooped to lift a
small box tied with ribbon, he mumbled, "That's for you.
It's some of Mama's things."

Then he picked up the two carpetbags that contained
his clothes, his collection of brass uniform buttons, what
little was left of last year's school supplies, some photographs taken before the war, and the family Bible—the
Bible with his parents' marriage date and all the children's
birth dates entered in his mother's beautiful script. And
all the dates of death, too. He himself had carefully printed
in the date of his mother's death just a week ago.

"What's in here?" asked Meg as she reached for a
long package wrapped in brown paper.

"That's my father's saber," Will answered, a note of pride creeping into his voice. "One of his friends brought it when he came to tell us that Papa'd been killed."

Aunt Ella led the way up the porch steps and into the house. After the bright afternoon sun, Will's eyes were slow to adjust to the dark interior, but he could see the big fireplace on one wall, the rocking chairs and trunklike chest arranged around it, and the large oak dining table near the front window. Through an open door on the other side of the room he saw a quilt-covered bed. He shut out the rising memories of the Winchester house and its large, bright, carpeted rooms filled with upholstered furniture. All that would be sold to pay Mama's debts. This was his home now.

Aunt Ella set her box on the table. Then she crossed the room, opened a narrow door, and started up the steep stairs to the attic. The low-ceilinged space had been partitioned into two sleeping rooms. She opened the door on the left and motioned Will to follow her inside.

In the dim light from the window at the gable end of the room, he saw the neatly made bed with its sunburst patterned quilt, a chest, one chair, and a small table. A kerosene lantern stood on the table.

When Aunt Ella saw his glance come to rest on the table, she explained, "Before the war, Sam did his studying there."

"I'll do my studying there, too," Will said, setting down his carpetbags and taking the package from Meg.

Aunt Ella sighed. "There's been no school around here since the schoolmaster volunteered early in the war. The building's been boarded up ever since—you probably saw it there by the store when you drove in—and with times so hard I doubt there'll be money to hire a teacher this year."

No school in the fall? Will could hardly imagine not having school! After the academy he'd attended had closed because of the war, he'd gone to the classes one of the pastors had held in his home.

The sound of a door opening broke the silence. "It's Pa!" cried Meg, running down the narrow stairway.

Aunt Ella rested her hand on Will's arm. "Come meet your Uncle Jed."

His mouth went dry. In the flurry of meeting his cousin and aunt, he'd momentarily forgotten his dread of living in the same house with a traitor—or with a coward, rather, since his uncle hadn't actually helped the enemy.

What would a coward look like? Will wondered as he followed his aunt downstairs. Expecting to see a frail, stoop-shouldered excuse for a man, he was surprised to find a sturdy man with a broad chest and muscular arms listening to Meg's excited chatter.

"So this is our city cousin," the man said, striding across the room. His high forehead and the dark, appraising eyes below his bushy brows were the only part of his face not covered by a luxuriant brown beard.

Will stared at his uncle's outstretched hand. He couldn't shake hands with a man who had refused to fight for the Southern cause! But he couldn't offend the head of the family that was taking him in, either. Slowly, he raised his right hand and felt it engulfed in the man's strong grasp.

Then his uncle said, "There's two squirrels for you out in the kitchen, Ella."

"I'll make a stew to go with the poke greens Meg cut along the road this afternoon," Aunt Ella said, turning toward the door. "You can bring me some wood for the fire, Will."

Glad to leave the house and his uncle, Will started for the woodshed. He gathered up an armload of split logs, choosing oak and locust to make the fire last.

His aunt smiled her thanks as he stacked the wood beside the stone fireplace that covered the north wall of the summer kitchen. "Now you can get me a potato from the cellar," she said, fanning the small flame she had coaxed from the embers.

Lifting the trap door in the far corner, Will could barely make out a ladder that led into the pitch blackness below.

"The lantern's on the shelf behind you," Aunt Ella said.

He raised the glass chimney, and his aunt touched the wick with a burning broom straw she'd lit at the fire. Then, carefully holding the lantern, he felt his way down the ladder. Will breathed in the earthy smell and savored the sudden coolness as his eyes passed over the shelves of empty canning jars and came to rest on the vegetable bins. He chose the largest of the wrinkled potatoes that covered the bottom of one bin and took it to his aunt.

"I'll split you some kindling now," Will said.

He found a hatchet, chose a piece of pine wood, and seated himself on a stump outside the woodshed. As he began to splinter off strips of wood, Meg joined him.

"Didn't you have slaves to do that sort of work?" she asked.

Will couldn't tell whether she was being sarcastic or not, but he decided to give her the benefit of the doubt. "We had three slaves," he said. "Callie was our cook, and Lizzy looked after the house. Fred did the outside work. He took care of our horses and split the wood and made the garden."

"Did the army get your horses, too?" asked Meg.

"My father was in the cavalry, so he and Fred took the horses."

Meg's eyes widened. "Did Fred go in the cavalry?"

"Fred went with my father, to look after him and the horses."

"But I thought—"

Will interrupted her. "You thought all slaves wanted to run away from their cruel masters, didn't you?" he challenged.

She nodded, her eyes not leaving his face.

"Well, that was true on a lot of big plantations farther south, but some slaves were well treated and cared about their families." Will shaved off more pine splinters. "Our Lizzy looked after Betsy and Eleanor when they were sick. She cried as hard as Mama did when they died."

Tracing a curve in the dust with her bare toe, Meg said simply, "My little sister died, too."

"You mean Beth?" Will said, looking up in surprise.

"She died during the war. After your mother started sending back Ma's letters without even opening them." Meg's voice was cold, and her eyes narrowed.

Will frowned. He hadn't known about that! He got up and went to the woodshed for another log.

"How did Beth die?" he asked when he came back. "Did she catch diphtheria?"

Meg shook her head. "Rebel scouts took our cow, and without any milk, she sickened. Wasted away, Ma said." She sighed. "I still miss her sometimes." Then, as an afterthought, she added, "Bessie was such a good milk cow, it seemed a shame to turn her to beef."

Will felt a wave of anger surge through him. "You should think of Nell and Bessie as your family's contribution to the war, since your father wouldn't fight," he said in a voice that was deadly quiet.

Meg's hands tightened into fists. "Pa saw no need to go to war so that rich people could keep their slaves!" she said.

Will dropped the hatchet and stood up to face his adversary. "Don't you know anything? The war wasn't about slavery—it was about states' rights! People in the South were tired of being told what to do by a govern-

ment hundreds of miles away in Washington. They wanted to live under laws made by their own state governments instead. The war was about states' rights, Meg."

"They just said that so men who didn't own slaves would fight in it!" Meg shot back. "Anyway, people's rights are more important than states' rights, and Pa had the right to decide not to fight in the war!"

Will looked scornfully at his cousin. "If men had the right to decide whether or not to fight when their country's at war, there wouldn't be any armies," he said.

Meg met his gaze. "I know of two armies we'd both have been a lot better off without," she said. Then she turned and walked back to the house, her head held high.

Will muttered an oath he'd learned from a young officer who had been quartered in their house one of the times Winchester was in Confederate hands. Then he scooped up an armload of kindling and headed for the summer kitchen.

Will was glad when the evening meal was over, even though he was still hungry. He knew he was stretching the family's meager food supply, and he was ill at ease in spite of his aunt's attempts to make him feel welcome.

He excused himself and climbed the stairs to his attic room. First he put his clothes in the chest and arranged the family Bible, his copybook with its few precious blank sheets, and his pen and ink bottle on the table under the window. Trying not to think about an autumn without school, he slipped his slate into the chest and tucked it under his clothes.

Will hesitated a moment, holding his small package of family photographs. Then, resolutely, he put them with his slate at the bottom of the chest. That done, he found a nail in the wall where he could hang his father's saber and the pouch of uniform buttons he'd collected from the battlefields and army camps near town. Then he threw himself across the bed.

He felt at ease with Aunt Ella and he guessed he'd learn to get along with Meg. Already they seemed almost like family, probably because they reminded him of Mama and Betsy. But he knew he'd never feel comfortable around his uncle. Imagine the son of a Confederate cavalry officer having to accept charity from such a man! He'd be courteous, and he'd help out all he could to make up for being an extra mouth to feed. But he'd never call him Uncle Jed. Never!

With that decided, Will flopped over on his stomach and fell into an exhausted sleep.

Thinking About It

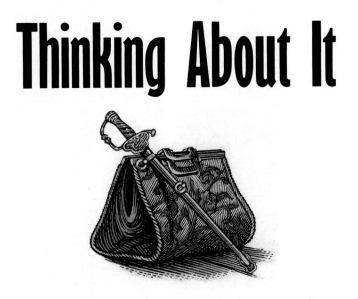

1. Although the story takes place over a hundred years ago, it lifts a curtain so you can examine the past. As you read it, what could you *see* most clearly? What conflicts could you feel?

2. Will must make his life in this new home. What clues in the story can you find to suggest what will happen?

3. At some point, Will and Uncle Jed will have to confront each other and get everything "out on the table." What will each say? Who do you think would have the more convincing argument?

Another Book About a Civil War Adventure

Will never fought in the Civil War, but Ransom, in *Red Cap* by G. Clifton Wisler, joined the Union army as a drummer boy at the age of thirteen. After two years of fighting, he was captured and sent to the horrible Confederate prison at Andersonville, Georgia. This story of terrible times and bravery is based on the true story of Ransom J. Powell, called Red Cap by his fellow soldiers.

So I Became a Soldier

BY JIM MURPHY

When word of Fort Sumter's fall reached him in Washington, President Abraham Lincoln acted quickly, issuing a call for seventy-five thousand volunteers to put down the insurrection. News of the President's call to arms spread with surprising speed—by telegraph, newspaper headlines, and word of mouth. Thomas Galway was fifteen years old and living in Cleveland, Ohio, when he heard.

"As I was coming from Mass this morning," Galway wrote in his journal, "I saw bulletins posted everywhere announcing the bombardment of Fort Sumter. Large crowds were gathered in front of each bulletin board, people peering over one another's head to catch a bit of the news. All seemed of one mind. Everyone talked of war."

Over in Indiana, fourteen-year-old Theodore Upson was working in the cornfield with his father when a neighbor came by. "William Cory came across the field (he had been to town after the Mail). He was excited and said, 'the Rebs have fired upon and taken Fort Sumpter.' Father got white and couldn't say a word.

"William said, 'The President will soon fix them. He has called for 75,000 men and is going to blocade their ports, and just as soon as those fellows find out that the North means business they will get down off their high horse.'"

Much the same was happening in the South. Newspapers hailed the victory at Sumter and predicted that the North would not risk any sort of military action. Public meetings were held to whip up support for the Confederate government.

T. G. Barker, then just thirteen, was attending a small private school in South Carolina. "We were in class," Barker remembered, "all bent over our books, when Headmaster Hammond entered. He did not knock to announce himself, which was unusual, and he did not speak to our teacher either. This was also unusual. He went instead to the middle of the room and said in a serious voice: 'We have had word this morning. Fort Sumter has surrendered and is now a part of the Confederate States of America.' Then he smiled. A second passed and not a sound. Then, as if shot from a cannon, the class stood as one and cheered Hooray! Hooray!"

The political and social causes of the war were numerous and complex, and still produce arguments among historians. Certainly, the profound cultural differences between the North and South were a factor, as were their opposing views on the issue of states' rights. And there is little doubt that an important element of the split was the institution of slavery. Many in the North saw slavery as evil and wanted it abolished completely. Others would accept slavery if it could be confined to the South or if the South agreed to phase it out over a number of years.

For its part, the South viewed slavery as vital to its economic survival. Agriculture, especially the growing of cotton, was its most important business. Slavery provided the cheap labor needed to bring in crops at a profit. Without slavery, Southerners argued, their entire way of life would crumble and be destroyed.

Intensifying matters was the fact that Southern interests were trying to introduce slavery in the newly settled western regions. Many in the North felt that slavery had to be stopped before it had a chance to spread and take hold in the West. As far as Southerners were concerned, the federal government was nothing more than an interfering bully trying to force its views on them.

The slavery question was not a new one at all. It had been discussed and debated, argued and fumed over for nearly fifty years. Tempers were frayed to the point of exploding, and fights had even taken place on the floor of the Senate. When war actually broke out, it was like a pressure-release valve. At last, the country seemed to sigh with relief, something concrete was finally going to settle the dispute.

The result on both sides was an enthusiastic rush to enlist. Men crowded the recruitment centers in the nearest cities or signed on with locally organized units. Emotions ran so high that everywhere enlistment quotas were being met and surpassed easily. Caught up in all of this were boys.

Generally, boys from the North did not join the army because they felt a burning desire to stamp out slavery. One boy's comment about slavery is fairly typical: "I do not know anything about it, whether it is a good thing or a bad thing," he wrote in a letter, "and when talk gets around to it I say very little." Many joined because they wanted to take the defiant South and "set them straight." But most signed up for a simpler reason—to escape the boring routine of farm life and take part in an exciting adventure.

The same spirit of adventure and glory motivated Southern boys as well. A Mississippi recruit said he had

Photograph courtesy
of Chicago Historical Society

joined "to fight the Yankies—all fun and frolic." But underneath the festive attitude was another, deeply felt reason for serving—to defend their homes from a large invading army. One Southern boy made his feelings clear, "I reather die then be com a Slave to the North."

Each side had recruitment rules that expressly banned boys from joining and fighting. At the start of the war, for instance, the Union held that a recruit had to be at least eighteen years old. In spite of this, a tall fourteen- or fifteen-year-old could easily blend into a crowd of men and slip through in the hurry to form a unit. Those questioned about their age might be able to bluff their way past a wary recruiting sergeant. Anyway, how would a recruiter check on an applicant's facts? The standard forms of identification we have today, such as driver's license, social security number, and credit cards, did not exist back then. There were no computers or telephones, either, so verifying someone's birthday was nearly impossible.

By far the easiest way for a boy to slip into the army was as a musician, especially as a drummer or bugler.

These were considered nonfighting positions, so recruiters often allowed a boy to sign on without worrying about his age. The Union army alone had need of over forty thousand musicians, while an estimated twenty thousand served for the South.

Many boys found it surprisingly simple to enlist for duty that would take them into the thick of the fighting. Thomas Galway did. The day after the surrender of Fort Sumter, Galway visited a nearby armory run by a group called the Cleveland Grays. "But they did not seem to me to be the sort of stuff that soldiers are made of, so I went away." That evening, "I went to the armory of the Hibernian Guards. They seemed to like me, and I liked them. So together with Jim Butler and Jim O'Reilly, I enlisted with them. My name was the first on the company's roll to enlist. I didn't tell them that I was only fifteen. So I became a soldier."

 On occasion, a boy would enter with the blessings of one or both parents. Ned Hutter went to join the Confederate army near his hometown in Mississippi. When the recruitment officer asked his age, Ned told him the truth: "'I am sixteen next June,' I said. . . . The officer ordered me out of line and my father, who was behind me, stepped to the table. 'He can work as steady as any man,' my father explained. 'And he can shoot as straight as any who has been signed today. I am the boy's father.' It must have been the way he said the words . . . [because] the officer handed me the pen and ordered, 'sign here.'"

Such support was rare, however, and most boys had to get in by less honest means. A fifteen-year-old Wisconsin boy, Elisha Stockwell, Jr., was one of them. "We heard there was going to be a war meeting at our little log school house," Stockwell recalled. "I went to the meeting and when they called for volunteers, Harrison Maxon (21), Edgar Houghton (16), and myself, put our names down. . . . My father was there and objected to my going, so they scratched my name out, which humiliated me somewhat. My sister gave me a severe calling down . . . for exposing my ignorance before the public, and called me a little snotty boy, which raised my anger. I told her, 'Never mind, I'll go and show you that I am not the little boy you think I am.'"

Elisha's hurt and anger calmed after his sister and mother apologized for what had been said. He even promised not to enlist again if he could attend school that winter. They agreed, and Elisha put aside his zeal to fight the Confederacy.

Unfortunately, Elisha's father had other plans for Elisha's winter. He'd signed up himself and his son to burn charcoal, a tedious, dirty, and backbreaking job. When Elisha learned this, he devised a new plan to enlist. First he told his parents he was going to a dance in town. Then he persuaded a friend's father, a captain in the Union army, to accompany him to a nearby recruitment center.

"The Captain got me in by my lying a little, as I told the recruiting officer I didn't know just how old I was but thought I was eighteen. He didn't measure my height, but called me five feet, five inches high. I wasn't that tall two years later when I re-enlisted, but they let it go, so the records show that as my height."

Elisha went home to gather up some clothes and found his sister in the kitchen preparing dinner. He did not mention anything about fighting for the Union, and after a brief conversation, "I told her I had to go down town. She said, 'Hurry back, for dinner will soon be ready.' But I didn't get back [home] for two years."

THINKING ABOUT IT

1 If you had been a younger brother or sister of one of the boys going off to fight, what would you have said to him? Why?

2 This selection is not historical fiction. But the author has used techniques to make it interesting. What are they? How would you read the article to make the most of these techniques?

3 Cast yourself in this article. If you had lived in the times it describes, who might you have been? What might you have said or written that could be quoted in a magazine article?

Another Book About an American Venture

True, boys and young men went off to fight the war, but young women did, too. *Gentle Annie* by Mary Francis Shura tells of Anna Blair Etheridge, who at sixteen joined her Michigan regiment as a laundress and nurse and served for four years in the front line.

Expedition to the Pacific

BY RHODA BLUMBERG

n expedition into mysterious lands beyond the boundaries of the United States!

American explorers would cross the nation's western border—the Mississippi River—then paddle, row, and sail their way across the middle of the continent to the Pacific Ocean. The Mississippi, Missouri, and Columbia Rivers would act as one continuous waterway. If the Missouri didn't connect with the Columbia, the explorers would carry their canoes for a short distance, from one river to another.

President Thomas Jefferson proposed this expedition in a secret message to Congress on January 18, 1803. Jefferson's

ideas didn't sound ridiculous because at that time many scientists were certain that these major American rivers flowed into one another.

In 1803, most of the West was as mysterious as Mars. It was an uncharted, blank space on all maps. Distances were underestimated and deserts unknown. People weren't even aware of the enormous height and width of the Rocky Mountains.

Foreign powers were competing for lands west of the Mississippi. Spain had stretched her Mexican borders north, and west to California. France owned a vast area on the west side of the Mississippi, just across from United States territory. Russia, having colonized Alaska, had an eye on the California coast. England posed the gravest threat. Even though the colonists had won the American Revolution in 1783, the British still had forts and trading posts on United States territory in 1803. Their trappers and traders worked south of the Great Lakes, where they monopolized trade with the Indians, bartering goods and guns for furs.

─────────── NEED FOR EXPLORATION ───────────

*T*homas Jefferson was especially alarmed after reading a book by Alexander Mackenzie, a Scottish fur trader who had crossed Canada and reached the Pacific Ocean in 1793. In his book, *Voyages from Montreal,* Mackenzie urged the British government to set up forts and trading posts across the continent and along the Pacific Coast.

Jefferson was convinced that a United States expedition was urgent. The Americans must prevent the English from claiming new territories on the American continent.[1]

─────────────────────

[1] Mackenzie's route to the Pacific was too difficult to be used for trade. His book, *Voyages from Montreal,* was published in 1801, read by Jefferson in 1803, and carried as a reference book by the Lewis and Clark expedition.

In his message to Congress, the President didn't mention the nation's need to control the continent. Congressmen were probably expected to read between the lines. Jefferson merely stated that an expedition was necessary for "extending the external commerce of the United States."[2]

Commerce was indeed one of Jefferson's important goals. Trapping and trading for furs were important to the nation's economy. By winning the West, the United States would find new sources of furs. American pelts were sold not only in Europe but also in Asia. Sea captains from America's East Coast enjoyed a fabulously profitable trade with China, where they bartered furs and other items for tea, silks, and porcelains (known as "chinaware").

However, to reach the Orient, Yankee skippers had to travel around South America, endangering their ships in the treacherous waters of Cape Horn.

If Jefferson's expedition provided a shortcut across America, eastern merchants could send their cargoes to and from the Pacific by river. Then, ships docked and waiting on the West Coast could sail to and from the Orient.

In addition to political and commercial aims, the President expected the explorers to contribute new information about nature and native American people.

Jefferson referred to his proposed expedition as a "literary pursuit." By "literary," he meant *scientific;* by "pursuit," *quest for knowledge.* He realized that some Senators and Congressmen mocked his ideas and viewed the West as a worthless wasteland. Therefore, he asked Congress for only $2,500 to finance his "Voyage of Dis-

[2]Donald Jackson, ed., *Letters of the Lewis and Clark Expedition with Related Documents 1783–1854* (Urbana: University of Illinois Press, 1962), Message to Congress, No. 8, 10–14.

covery." The low estimate guaranteed that political opponents would not veto his proposal. The President assured Congress that his mission could be accomplished by "an intelligent officer with ten or twelve chosen men."[3]

*T*he "intelligent officer" chosen to command Jefferson's "literary pursuit" was Meriwether Lewis. Lewis was twenty-eight years old and had served as the President's personal secretary for two years. Lewis had never attended college, but he had received a superb education at the White House with Jefferson. Lewis used the President's extensive library, which had books on a staggering number of subjects, ranging from astronomy to zoology.

Jefferson declared that politics was his "duty," but natural history his "passion."[4] He conveyed this passion to Lewis, and boasted that his secretary had developed a talent for observing plants and animals.

Lewis helped the President plot a cross-country exploration. Although Jefferson had never been more than fifty miles west of Monticello, Virginia, he expected to advise and guide his secretary through an unknown wilderness. The President even invented a secret code, to be used whenever he and Lewis corresponded. Messengers were supposed to find their way to and from Washington, D.C., with reports that only Lewis and Jefferson could decipher. The White House would act as a control center for adventurers in unknown space. The code, however, was never used. It turned out to be impossible to dispatch messengers from the western wilderness to Washington.

[3]Ibid., Message to Congress, No. 8, 10–14.

[4]The President measured and recorded rainfall, temperature, and wind direction; described the migrations of birds; noted the dates that plants flowered and had fruits; jotted down the times he noticed a new insect, a fresh leaf, spring's first frog croak, summer's first firefly, and autumn's last-heard katydid.

To prepare Lewis for the great expedition, Jefferson sent his secretary to see scholars in Philadelphia. In one month, Lewis was given cram courses in science. The botanist Benjamin Smith Barton taught him the art of preserving plants and furnished notes on zoology and Indian history. The astronomer Caspar Wistar talked not only about constellations, but about fossils as well. He urged Lewis to collect bones and warned him to watch out for living mammoths—and for "Great Claw" (a giant sloth). It was possible, he claimed, that these monsters might be roaming about in the uncharted West.

Dr. Benjamin Rush, the country's outstanding physician, assembled a medicine kit and gave Lewis implements for bleeding and operating on patients. He also supplied fifty dozen of his own pills—laxatives that were to become known as "Rush's thunderbolts."

Because the explorers would have to doctor themselves, Rush also supplied written rules "for the Preservation of his [Lewis's] Health and of those who were to accompany him":

- *When fatigued, lie down for two whole hours.*

- *Wash your feet in cold water every morning.* [Jefferson always did!]

- *When your feet are chilled wash them with "a little spirits"* [liquor].

- *During difficult marches eat very little to avoid becoming overtired.*[5]

---

[5]Dr. Rush might have been dismayed to learn that the explorers didn't take time out during the day for two-hour naps, that they would not think of soaking their feet in liquor that the group preferred to drink, and that they didn't eat sparingly in order to have energy.

Dr. Rush also prepared a lengthy questionnaire for Lewis about the health of the Indians they would meet: their diseases, remedies, eating habits, lifespans. Lewis was even expected to check the pulse rate of children and adults "in the morning, at noon, and at night before and after eating."[6]

Before leaving Philadelphia, Lewis bought over a ton of supplies that included gifts for Indians. There were beads, buttons, curtain rings (to adorn fingers and ears), ruffled shirts, red fabrics, red-handled knives, and red paint for decorating bodies. Tomahawks and knives were also included as gifts.

Camp supplies, clothing, and weapons had to be purchased. With the help of a professional cook, Lewis concocted 150 pounds of "portable soup"—a dried, instant broth that tasted terrible, but would be used if the explorers ran short of food.

Scientific instruments such as quadrants, compasses, and magnifying devices were also on the shopping list. And there were books on mineralogy, botany, history, anatomy, and astronomy that Lewis borrowed or bought. A four-volume dictionary was part of a weighty library to be lugged, round trip, from coast to coast.

Lewis designed a collapsible canoe. The boat's frame came apart for carrying, weighed about one hundred pounds, and could be assembled easily. It was supposed to carry a ton of gear. Lewis was proud of his ingenious invention. He named his creation "The Experiment."

Wagons transported supplies and purchases to Pittsburgh, where they were loaded on a boat for shipment down the Ohio River. From there they were sent up the Mississippi to St. Louis.

---

[6]Rush asked if Indian ceremonies were like those of the Jews. This question was included because many people believed that Indians were descended from the Lost Tribes of Israel. See Jackson, *Letters of the Lewis and Clark Expedition*, Benjamin Rush to Lewis, No. 8, 50.

*P*resident Jefferson issued official instructions for Lewis. He stressed that the purpose of the expedition was to discover a direct water route to the Pacific Ocean. Lewis was also obligated to make detailed reports about soil, vegetation, fossils, minerals, climate, mammals, insects, birds, and reptiles. All observations were "to be taken with great pains & accuracy, to be entered distinctly and intelligibly" into an official log of the expedition.

The President urged Lewis to tell Indians of "our wish to be neighborly, friendly, and useful to them." He stressed that it was important to obtain the names of Indian nations, their numbers, and "the articles of trade they may need or furnish." As the ultimate goodwill gesture, Lewis was to invite Indian chiefs to visit Washington, D.C., as guests of the United States government.[7]

When Jefferson issued these official instructions on June 20, 1803, he had no idea that American diplomats in Paris had already purchased a huge chunk of North America. Napoleon sold France's Louisiana Territory at the bargain price of 15 million dollars. The great conqueror needed money for his European campaigns. This was history's greatest real estate deal. For four cents an acre, the United States doubled its size.[8]

The purchase agreement was dated April 30, 1803, but the news did not reach Jefferson until July. The President was relieved. Napoleon the Great was no longer his nation's unwanted neighbor. The expedition need no longer be viewed as an undercover intelligence mission on foreign soil. The men would openly explore territory now owned by the United States. However, they would still in-

[7]Ibid., Jefferson's Instructions to Lewis, No. 47, 61.
[8]The Louisiana Territory is equal to about one-third the area of the United States today (excluding Alaska and Hawaii).

vade no-man's land after they reached the foothills of the Rocky Mountains.

————————— WILLIAM CLARK —————————

*F*aced with the challenge of leading men into the unknown, Lewis decided he wanted his friend, thirty-three-year-old William Clark, as co-leader of the expedition.

Before Lewis had been appointed Jefferson's secretary, he had served in the army with Clark. Both men had been trained by General "Mad Anthony" Wayne, a fanatic who demanded excessive inspections, drills, and discipline. Clark was an experienced woodsman, a good surveyor, and a fine leader. At one time he had been Lewis's commanding officer.

Clark had retired from the army and was managing his family's farm in Kentucky when he received the letter from Lewis asking him to become co-captain of the expedition. Eager for action, Clark replied that he looked forward to the "dangers, difficulties, and fatigues," and assured Lewis that "no man lives whith whome I perfur to undertake such a Trip as yourself."[9]

Clark's acceptance brightened for Lewis an aggravating summer spent in Pittsburgh. He was waiting for boatbuilders ("incorrigible drunkards") who took their time completing a fifty-five-foot barge with sails, called a keelboat.

Lewis was so impatient to get going that on August 31, 1803, only four hours after the long-overdue boat was finished, he launched it down the Ohio. Half a dozen recruits from the army, a river pilot, and three men whose qualifications were "on trial" accompanied him. Clark, Clark's slave, York, and more volunteer soldiers came aboard at Louisville, Kentucky.

[9]See Jackson, *Letters of the Lewis and Clark Expedition*, Clark to Lewis, No. 74, 110.

Thinking About It

1 Have you ever planned a trip—even if it was just to go to a local park? How did you plan it? How was your planning similar to and different from the planning for the Lewis and Clark expedition?

2 Look again at the footnotes in the selection. Why does a writer use footnotes? Which ones are helpful? Explain why.

3 What is the end of the expedition? *Where* did it end and *what happened* to the explorers? What is the best way to find out? What are the best ways to reveal the information to someone to interest her or him?

Sacagawea

BY SCOTT O'DELL

Six months
after the Lewis and Clark expedition got
under way, the explorers realized they
needed to prepare for winter. They built
Fort Mandan—near present-day
Bismarck, North Dakota—as their winter headquarters.

Then they hired as a guide a French
trader, Toussaint Charbonneau, and
Sacagawea, his Shoshone Indian wife.
The year has been extremely eventful for
Sacagawea: she was captured by Minnetaree warriors during a raid on her
Shoshone village; Charbonneau won her
from her intended husband Red Hawk
in a game of chance; she was married to
Charbonneau; she is now pregnant with
her first child and facing a dangerous
journey halfway across North America.

Captain Clark changed my life. He changed everything. More than the slave hunters who came and took me from my home. More than Toussaint Charbonneau, who won me in the dreadful Hand Game. I say this before my Guardian Spirit, who may make me dead forever if I do not speak the truth.

It happened in this way. When the captains learned that Charbonneau had traded on the rivers for many years, as far to the north and west as the home of the Assiniboins and the Blackfeet and the Nez Percé, they hired him as a guide to help George Drewyer interpret Indian words for them.

They were building a camp farther along the river, where there were wide groves of cottonwood trees to use for timber. The men needed shelter against the cold. And besides this, the captains had heard that the Sioux were planning an attack sometime during the winter.

The men built a strong camp. It had two rows of huts joined together at one end, which were guarded by walls and two swivel guns. It was so strong they called it a fort, Fort Mandan—Mandan because the land belonged to the Mandan people, who were at peace with the Minnetarees.

I wanted to stay where I was, but Captain Clark made us move into the fort.

"You'll be safe here at Fort Mandan," he said. "And you can visit your Minnetaree friends anytime you wish. They're not far away."

Charbonneau told me about the pact with Captain Clark the day he was hired and we moved into the fort. He showed me the paper the captain had written on.

Even more wonderful was what Captain Clark said to Drewyer, who said to me, "The captain is hiring you just as much as your husband. He's learned that you are a Shoshone. He knows that the Shoshone live in the mountains, where he needs to travel, and that they own many fine horses, which he needs to buy. Is it true about the horses?"

"Yes," I said. "The Shoshone have many fine horses. They will wish to sell some, I think."

C aptain Clark wanted to know if my father was a big man in the tribe. He also wished to know my name.

I told Drewyer my name was Sacagawea and that my father was a chieftain.

Captain Clark looked at me. "Sacagawea?" He spoke the name slowly and frowned.

He kept looking at me. He spoke to George Drewyer, who said, "He does not like the sound of Sacagawea. He wishes to call you Janey. You look like a girl he knew someplace whose name was Janey. So Janey is what he wishes to call you from this day on."

Captain Clark asked him to ask me if I liked the name.

I said "Janey" to myself. I said the name out loud. It was hard to say. It had a strange sound in my mouth.

Captain Clark was watching, waiting to see if I liked it, so I nodded my head and smiled. I did not tell him that I had another name besides Sacagawea, a secret name, which I seldom used because if you say your real name too much, it gets worn away and loses its magic.

"Janey," Captain Clark said and went on speaking fast in his language. When he was done Drewyer told me what he had said.

"The captain sees that you are going to have a baby soon. He wonders if you will be able to make the long journey. To places no white man has ever been. Over the high mountains and beyond to the big water. He wants you to go because you can help him with the horses when he comes to the land of the Shoshone. But he wonders about the baby."

I told the captain not to worry. With the baby safe on my back I would go anywhere he went, over the mountains to the big water, anywhere. The captain smiled and went away and I did not see him again until the night my son was born.

inter came. The sun was a white ghost in the sky. It went down early and night came fast. There was no one around, except children playing, the day I fell down in pain and dragged myself to the fire and lay there and struggled for breath.

Blue Sky[1] came. She got me into bed. I remember she put a deerskin blanket over me and a bearskin over that. I do not remember anything else until she and George Drewyer were standing beside the bed, talking to Captain Clark.

I asked where Charbonneau was. Blue Sky said he had gone to haul wood and he would be back in the morning sometime.

They went on talking, but the words sounded far away. There was a long silence. Everyone was silent, even the children. The fire was making shadows on the roof. Strange faces with gaping mouths were looking at me. Then they began to scream and I screamed back at them with all the breath I had.

I heard Blue Sky say to someone in Minnetaree, "What is to be done? She is dying."

Dying? The word soothed my pain somehow. I lay quiet. I waited for my Guardian Spirit to speak. I waited for the voices of those who were no longer living, my mother and my friends in the land of the Shoshone. I felt very calm.

[1]Wife of the Mandan chief, Black Moccasin

Captain Clark spoke to Drewyer, who spoke to Blue Sky: "The captain has something he would like to do. He has tried it before. Sometimes it works and sometimes it does not work."

"What is it?" Blue Sky said.

"He has the rattle from a rattlesnake in his pocket and he wants to break up two of its rings. Make small pieces of them. Put them in a little water and make her swallow."

"Why not," Blue Sky said. "She is dying."

The stuff had no taste, only a scratchy feeling as it went down, but it sent me to sleep. When I woke up it was daylight and the baby was being born.

Charbonneau came soon after. He had heard the news and strode in singing. He wanted to know whether he had a son or a daughter.

"A son," I said. "We can name him Meeko."

"Meeko? What does something like that mean?"

"Little Brown Squirrel."

Charbonneau tossed his head. "No Meeko. No brown squirrel. Jean Baptiste Charbonneau," he said.

Captain Clark thought for a while. "Pompey is a fine name. Pompey Charbonneau."

Why he chose this name he did not say. It had a good sound, but not as good as Meeko; so I called my son Meeko. Not so loud that either of the men could hear it.

Drewyer said, "Captain Clark wants to know when you will be strong enough to go."

"Go now," Charbonneau said. "This girl strong Indian girl. Go now."

"A week yet. When the ice melts on the river," Captain Clark said.

He came back the next day and for five days to see how I felt. On the last day he brought Captain Lewis.

Captain Lewis had an animal with him. At first I

thought it was a young buffalo. Then it came up and rubbed against me and I saw that it was a dog. But it was a dog as big as a young buffalo. It was shaggy and brown and had big gray-brown eyes. Drewyer said that its name was Scannon and that it came from a place called Newfoundland, wherever that was.

After he had rubbed against me for a while and pushed me from side to side, Scannon went over and sniffed at Meeko. The baby did not like the wet nose, but that made no difference to Scannon. He sniffed anyhow.

That day Captain Clark decided that I should learn some of the words he spoke.

That day he taught me to count from one to twenty in the white man's tongue. The next time he taught me the names of the days, and how many days made a week, and how many weeks made a month. "Night" was a new word for me. In Shoshone we always called the night a "sleep." For instance, "We traveled for six sleeps." Now I could say we traveled for six nights.

Scarcely a day went by from this time to the end of the journey that I failed to learn ten words of the white man's language. Sometimes I learned twenty words and more.

———◆—◇—◆———

Meeko liked the cradleboard I made for him. He smiled the first time I put him in it. And when I took him out he screwed up his face.

This was good. Some babies in the Mandan village disliked the cradleboards. This was a big burden, because their mothers had to carry them around whatever they were doing.

With me, while I got things together for the long journey—I made an extra pair of moccasins, as well as leggings—all I had to do was to hang Meeko and his fur-lined cradleboard on a pole beside me. I never had to worry about him until it was feeding time.

When the ice broke up I was ready. But just three days before we were to leave, three traders from Canada came to the village and asked to talk to Charbonneau.

They talked for a long time. Afterward, he told me that the Canada men worked for the Northwest Company and were afraid that the Americans would ruin their trade with the Indians.

That night he woke me to say that there were many things about the journey he did not like.

"What?" I asked him. "What are they?"

"Money," he said. "Money not enough. Other things. High mountains, very high. I hear from old trader Le Blanc, long time ago. Also, many Indians. Like Assiniboins and Blackfeet. Unfriendly people, these. Slit throat, take scalp quick."

"But you gave a promise to the captains," I said.

Otter Woman[2] was awake now. For a long time she had been telling me that it was foolish to go on such a dangerous journey among bad people and for such poor pay.

Sleepily, she said to him, "Do not listen. Go and say, 'Charbonneau wishes more money. Other things, too.'"

"I tell them," he said. "Charbonneau comes back if Charbonneau wishes. Anytime, if Toussaint Charbonneau wishes, he comes back."

"Tell them," Otter Woman said.

From the day Charbonneau was hired, the thought of going into the mountains where my people lived and seeing them again warmed my heart. The thought of the

[2]Charbonneau's other wife

journey itself, what it was about, what Captain Clark and Captain Lewis sought, and wherever the mysterious journey led, excited me.

"You gave a promise," I said. "You cannot quit now."

He went the next morning to talk to the captains. At nightfall he returned, angry and sullen, to say that he had a fight with them.

"I tell them goodbye," he said. "No more journey. Goodbye, Captain Clark, goodbye, Captain Lewis. Goodbye."

he next day the truth came out. The captains had told him to leave and not come back. Captain Clark even said that it was me he really wanted. Not as a guide, but as someone who could help him buy horses and find his way through the country of the Shoshone.

Charbonneau brooded for a while. I begged him to go and talk to the captains again.

"Why do they want someone who quits somewhere along the trail if he feels like it?" I asked him. "If you were Captain Clark, would you want someone like that? And if you quit, it will give you a bad name on the river."

Otter Woman kept at him, too. But she did everything she could to keep him from going. She liked her easy life traveling from one village to another, visiting places and people. But I talked, too, and at last he went back to Captain Clark and said that he was not mad anymore. He would like to go with them now.

As soon as this was over, I put everything I had made during the long winter for myself and Meeko into a deerskin bag. I put the baby and his cradleboard on my back. I said goodbye to Otter Woman, who was very pleased to be left behind.

Every day Captain Clark made black marks in a thing he called a journal. He made the marks with a stick he dipped in black paint. He said the marks were words that told everything he had seen or heard or thought that day.

When I went down to the river, he was there, sitting in one of the big boats. The journal was in his lap. He motioned me to put down the bag and the cradleboard and to sit beside him. He opened the journal, wet the stick, and put it in my hand. He put his arm around my shoulder and took my hand and guided it over the paper.

These are the things that we put in the journal together:

Fort Mandan April the 7th 1805 Sunday, at 4 o'Clock PM, the boat, in which were 6 soldiers, 2 French-men and an Indian, all under the command of a corporal who had the charge of dispatches, &c.—and a canoe with 2 Frenchmen, set out down the river for St. Louis. At the same time we set out on our voyage up the river in 2 pirogues and 6 canoes.

That was all I wrote while Captain Clark guided my hand. I looked at the marks as they ran back and forth on the page. I felt very proud of myself. Not until much later, when I began to learn more about the white man's language, did I know what all the marks meant.

Captain Clark wrote some more in his journal.

I saw the word "Janey," the name he had given to me. He quickly sprinkled the words with sand to dry them off. I suppose they had something to do with me.

The big silver boat that looked like a gull went down the river. Captain Lewis fired his swivel guns to say goodbye to the Mandans and we went fast up the river.

Near nightfall everyone waded to shore and I was sent out to dig roots for supper. Both of the big boats, the pirogues, were stored with food, but Captain Clark planned to use it only if nothing could be found on land. I was sent out because Charbonneau had said when the captain hired him that he should have more money because I, his wife, knew how to gather berries and all kinds of roots.

Finding roots was easy. I had done it since I was a child.

The first thing to know is where to look. The best place is around piles of driftwood. You take a sharp stick and poke until you come upon a mouse hole. Always in the hole, except at the end of winter, you will find a nest of roots from the camas bush that the mice have stored up.

The roots are as big as your thumb, white and round. They are good tasting if they are cooked with deermeat or buffalo hump.

It was the end of winter and the mice had eaten most of their store, so I had to dig long after dark. I dug enough roots for more than three dozen men.

It is best when cooking camas roots to dig a pit and put hot stones on the bottom and cover them with willow branches and lay the roots on top. You put more branches on and heap them with earth. You build a fire and let it burn until you can tell by the good smells that the roots are done.

It takes almost two days to do this. Since the men were hungry, I just boiled the roots. I dug them and cooked them because I wanted to please Captain Clark.

Charbonneau was angry. He said to Captain Clark at supper, "Me and wife, Bird Girl, get no pay for cook. For talk. For guide. No cook."

"Janey wanted to dig the roots and cook them," Captain Clark said. "The men usually cook for themselves."

"Good," Charbonneau said. Afterward he said to me, "You no cook. Find roots, no cook. See?"

I was not displeased. To cook for three dozen hungry men was more than I could do.

We passed a Minnetaree village early the next morning, the one Le Borgne ruled over. The river runs narrow here past a low cliff and he was watching for us as we came out of the mist. He raised his hand and pointed at a huge pile of meat on the bank beside him.

"Buffalo," he shouted. "Welcome to good eating. Welcome, friends."

Captain Clark shouted back, but when Charbonneau, who was steering, turned toward shore, Captain Clark grabbed the rudder and kept us headed straight. It was well that he did. For when we floated by and left Le Borgne standing on the bank, a shower of arrows from the cliff fell upon us.

For the first time I wondered about Charbonneau. He had heard the horrible tales about Le Borgne. He knew that the one-eyed chieftain could not be trusted, that he hated the white men. Knowing this, why had Charbonneau tried to steer the boat ashore into the hands of an enemy?

nly a few days later, less than a week, I wondered even more about him. He was at the rudder of our pirogue when a gust of wind struck us and wrested the rudder from his grip. Instead of taking hold of the rudder again, he raised his hands and began to pray.

The other boats were farther up the river.

Cruzatte, the bowsman, shouted at Charbonneau, "Turn her, you fool!" Charbonneau was still praying. Cruzatte shouted again, "Turn her!"

Charbonneau was on his knees, clinging to the pirogue with one hand.

"Turn!" Cruzatte shouted again. "Turn her or I'll shoot you!"

He pointed a gun at Charbonneau's head.

Charbonneau pulled hard at the rudder, but the boat stayed sideways.

The sails flapped and we tilted. Water rushed in. It swept around my knees. The baby started to cry. I saw that the shore was not far away and that I could reach it. Then I saw that our stores had begun to drift out of the boat. Charbonneau watched them drift but did not move.

Cruzatte seized the rudder.

We were floating with the current now and around us in a wide circle the water was covered with the stores that had drifted out of the boat. I saw Captain Clark's journal and a wooden box that held something he valued. He took it out of the box every day, looked at it, and carefully put it back.

Someone shouted from the shore. Waves were beating so loud against the boat I could not make out what was said, but it had a warning sound. The cradleboard had loosened. I tightened the cord that bound it to my shoulders and let myself into the water. It came up higher than my waist.

The first thing I gathered in was the wooden box. Then I grasped the journal that I had written in once and Captain Clark wrote in almost every day. A wave broke over our heads and the baby began to cry, so I gave up and climbed back in the boat.

I got safely to land but we lost most of our medicine, gunpowder, flour, melon seeds that Captain Clark was going to plant somewhere, and many other things, besides some of our beads and presents for people along the way. But I saved his journal and the wooden box. He was pleased to see them when he came back that night.

"Good as new," he said, opening the box. "I have a small one, but this is by far the best."

"What is it?" I asked him.

"A compass. You can tell whether you are traveling north or south or east or west. Otherwise you get lost."

D·56

He was so pleased that he kissed me on the cheek and gave me a beautiful gift. It was an antelope belt sewn with rows of tiny blue beads. It was so beautiful my throat choked up and I couldn't thank him.

After supper I asked Charbonneau why he had not obeyed Cruzatte.

"Hear nothing," he said. "Hear wind, hear water. No hear Cruzatte."

A tight look around his mouth made me think he was telling a lie. He had heard Cruzatte.

"You think something?" he asked me, clenching his hands. "You think Charbonneau hear, huh?"

I shook my head.

I began to wonder. I remembered the day the traders had talked to him. How that night he had told me that they were afraid the Americans would ruin their business. How the next day he had told Captain Clark he would not go with him. And how, the very next day, he had changed his mind and decided to go.

Was it possible that he had some secret with the Canada traders? Had they hired him to make trouble?

"You think things?" he asked, still clenching his hands.

"Nothing," I said.

"You jump in river. Near drown. Jean Baptiste near drown. Jean Baptiste Charbonneau worth more than captains. More than Bird Girl. Anybody. See?"

"Yes," I said.

If his son meant that much to him, why had he tried to destroy the boat and take the chance that Meeko might drown? Why had he sat with his hands in the air and prayed, deaf to Cruzatte's commands? I did not dare to ask him.

"What you think?" he said. "You think Charbonneau hear Cruzatte, huh?"

"No."

"Good," he said and unclenched his fists. "Good."

 esides the other things, we lost all of our flour and most of the pemmican. It was a bad loss. Captain Clark said that now we had to live on the roots we gathered and the animals our hunters shot.

We saw no animals the next few days, except the many buffalo that had died in the ice during the winter and a bear that ran from our hunters. To the west where the prairie stretched farther than the eye could see, the banks were covered with flowering bushes. But it was much too early for berries. So I dug roots every night when we stopped and they were cooked with the last of the pemmican.

The river was shallow. Yet currents ran strong. Wading in mud up to their knees, stumbling over rocks and logs, the men pulled on ropes fastened to the bow of each boat. Men on the boats had long poles that they thrust into the water at the bow and stern.

If the wind blew right, sails were raised on the pirogues. But mostly the men clawed their way up the river. Those with the small canoes had less trouble, yet everyone suffered. Boiled camas root with a few shreds of pemmican was not enough for men who toiled so hard from dawn to nightfall.

Captain Lewis asked everyone to look for animals—antelope, bears, deer, or buffalo. He sent bands of hunters out to search both sides of the river.

Soon after the bad accident, a grizzly bear was sighted. It was shambling along the shore of a sandbar in the middle of the river, a sandbar like the one I had lived on when I fled from Le Borgne.

Bearmeat is not the best meat to be found, being tough to the teeth and musky on the tongue. Besides, bears are dangerous. But Captain Lewis had no choice. He sent Captain Clark out to bring back bearmeat.

Captain Clark, Sergeant Ordway, and a hunter got ready. As they were about to set off the grizzly came out of the bush with a cub.

"It is black luck to kill a bear that has a young one at her side," I said to Captain Clark.

He looked at me as if he thought there might be nothing in my head.

"It is black luck," I said.

"My men are hungry. What would you have us do, starve?"

"There are other bears, without young, to kill," I said.

"Where? We have traveled for nine days. This is the first we've had a chance to kill."

Charbonneau was in the water, pulling the boat ashore. He stopped and gave me a disgusted look. "Crazy talk," he said. "Crazy Shoshone talk."

The bear had seen us and had gone into the heavy brush in the center of the sandbar. She took the cub with her.

Captain Lewis called to Captain Clark, "Take your hunters and follow them." To Charbonneau he said, "Get back in the boat and stay. Watch what happens. Be ready to pull away should you need to!"

Two hunters waded to the sandbar and took up their places. With his rifle on his shoulder, Captain Clark stood not far from me on the shore.

The hunter at the far end of the sandbar fired into the brush. The bear came out, swaying her head from side to side. She glanced along the bank, first at the hunter whose gun was still smoking, then at Sergeant Ordway, then at Captain Clark.

I was wearing the belt of blue beads that Captain Clark had given me. It caught the sun. The bear's eyes fastened upon me. She was making up her mind which one of us to attack.

"Crazy bear," Charbonneau said, getting ready to put the boat back into the river. "Like crazy womans. What she do, no telling. Crazy."

I turned away so he would not see me. I closed my eyes and prayed. I asked the Great Spirit to spare the mother and her cub. I prayed that she would flee back into the brush. Night was coming on. If they did not kill her now, she would be safe. I prayed until I heard a second shot.

Captain Clark had fired his gun. He was wrapped in a cloud of yellow smoke. Dust spurted up from the bear's furry hide. She fell to her knees, but quickly she gathered herself and rose to her full height. She was taller than a tall man.

Someone shot and missed. The bear did not move. She was watching Captain Clark. He was the closest to her of the hunters, not ten short strides away. I saw the danger he was in. I must have uttered a warning, for Charbonneau became angry.

"Clark no child of Sacagawea," he said. "Clark no husband of Sacagawea. Why Sacagawea make big fuss?"

I did not answer him. This was the first time that I knew how I truly felt about Captain Clark. My heart beat so hard I could not have spoken if I wanted to.

The bear no longer stood on her hind legs. She was watching Captain Clark. He took out a paper tube with gunpowder in it and a ball. He tore the tube open with his teeth and poured powder into the pan. He crumpled the brown paper around the ball and put it into the barrel.

The bear sniffed the air. I think she smelled the bitter smell of the powder.

She moved toward him. She lifted her paws high at each step she took. It might have been the sounds the river made, but I was sure that I heard her claws crunch into the sand. There was blood running down her shoulder. She paused to lick it off.

The hunters fired twice and the bear fell. But while the hunters began to load their guns again, while Captain Clark finished loading his, the bear was on her feet once more. She staggered toward him. She growled with rage and her eyes were a fiery red.

The hunters shouted. "Run," I screamed as loud as I could.

I jumped out of the boat and waded into the river. The baby in his cradleboard was on my back. Captain Clark was in the river. He braced himself against the current and fired his gun. One of the hunters also fired.

When she was dragged out of the water and laid on the bank, the men found five bullets. One was sunk deep in her heart. The men said that her flesh was dry and stringy, yet they ate all of it that night. They were making up for the days without meat.

In the morning we left early. The cub stood at the edge of the brush, but Captain Lewis was in too much of a hurry to take time to hunt it down.

Thinking About It

1 The author tells you about Sacagawea through her thoughts and actions. What have you figured out about Sacagawea by the time you finish reading this part of her adventures?

2 "Sacagawea" is historical fiction, a story about characters who actually lived and an expedition that actually happened. Which parts may have been made up by the author? Find examples. Why might the author have mixed fact and fiction?

3 Do what Meriwether Lewis couldn't do: Send a report home to President Jefferson. What do you say in it?

Railroads

BY RUTHANNE LUM McCUNN

California became a state
two years after gold was
discovered. There was
plenty of work to be done
in building the new state.

One big project was to build a railroad
that would join the East Coast with the
West. The plan was for the Union Pacific to
lay track from the East while the Central
Pacific Railroad (headed by the "Big Four"
Crocker, Stanford, Hopkins and Hunting-
ton) started from the West. The government
promised the railroad companies anywhere
from $16,000 to $48,000 plus a grant of
land for every mile of road that was con-
structed. This was the beginning of a great
railroad race for power and profit.

At first, Charles Crocker had no
problem in hiring workmen because
shiploads of Irishmen were arriving in

San Francisco. However, railroad work was very dangerous and exhausting. The foremen complained that the
workers were often drunk and rowdy and constantly de-
manding higher wages. After each pay day, several
hundred workers would disappear.

 As a result, it took the Central Pacific
two years to lay only fifty miles of track.
Charles Crocker was worried. His
railroad company needed to work
faster but he couldn't get the laborers
he needed. In 1865, Crocker's
foreman, John H. Strobridge, could only get 800 laborers.
He needed 5,000. Crocker told Strobridge to hire Chinese.

The Chinese already had excellent work records with
another railroad company, the California Central which
had hired them to replace the white workers who left for
the gold mines in the 1850's. However, Strobridge refused to hire Chinese. He said, "I will not boss Chinese. I
will not be responsible for work done by Chinese laborers. I don't think they could build a railroad." Governor
Leland Stanford, one of the "Big Four," was also against
hiring Chinese laborers. In fact, he wanted the Chinese
excluded from California.

Finally, Crocker was so desperate that he forced
Strobridge to hire fifty Chinese as an experiment. They
worked so well that 3,000 more were hired. Governor
Stanford changed his attitude about the Chinese. In a report to President Andrew Johnson on October 10, 1865,
he wrote, "Without them (the Chinese) it would be impossible to complete the Western portion of this great
national enterprise within the time required by the
Acts of Congress."

At first, most Chinese workers were recruited from
the mining districts. Then contractors were sent to China
to bring back more laborers. Soon, four out of five work-

ers on the railroad were Chinese and construction moved ahead quickly.

When the railroad reached the High Sierras, the workers had many difficulties to overcome. The hardest part was to carve away big chunks of the mountains with explosives so track could be laid. But there was no place for even a foothold in the steep cliffs.

Chinese workers were lowered in baskets. They drilled holes for the explosives, lit the fuses and then swung out as far as they could to avoid the blast. Other workers quickly pulled up the ropes, but sometimes the baskets were not hauled up quickly enough, and the men were killed by the explosions. Sometimes the ropes broke, and the workers fell to their deaths.

Another problem was the snow. Entire work camps were buried to the rooftops in snow. The men burrowed through tunnels like moles. They breathed through air shafts and never saw daylight until spring. Occasionally, avalanches swept whole camps down the mountains. The bodies, still clutching their shovels, were not found until the following spring when the snows melted.

After the snows of the High Sierras came the scorching heat of the Nevada desert. Some of the Chinese tried to leave for other work. They were beaten, whipped and forced to stay.

Others complained about unfair working conditions. The Chinese were paid $26 a month without board while the white laborers received $35 a month plus board. The white workers also worked fewer hours and they were never used for the dangerous jobs.

Finally, 2,000 Chinese workers went on strike in 1867. They demanded the same work day and wages as white workers and the right to look for other work. Charles Crocker broke the strike by forcing the Chinese to go without food and water supplies until they went back to work.

The railroad between the West and East Coasts was finished in 1869. There were huge celebrations from coast to coast. The Chinese, however, were excluded from participating and they were not even mentioned during the ceremonies.

Nevertheless, the Chinese continued to build rail links throughout California, the Southwest and the Northwest.

Thinking About It

1. What do you think was the worst situation the Chinese had to face while building the railroads? Explain.

2. What picture do you get of people like Charles Crocker, John Strobridge, and the workers? How does the author make you see them?

3. Be one of the railroad builders. What would you say of your work and your accomplishment?

Spirits of the Railway

BY PAUL YEE

One summer many, many years ago, heavy floodwaters suddenly swept through south China again. Farmer Chu and his family fled to high ground and wept as the rising river drowned their rice crops, their chickens and their water buffalo.

With their food and farm gone, Farmer Chu went to town to look for work. But a thousand other starving peasants were already there. So when he

heard there was work across the ocean in the New World, he borrowed some money, bought a ticket, and off he sailed.

Long months passed as his family waited to hear from him. Farmer Chu's wife fell ill from worry and weariness. From her hard board bed she called out her husband's name over and over, until at last her eldest son borrowed money to cross the Pacific in search of his father.

For two months, young Chu listened to waves batter the groaning planks of the ship as it crossed the ocean. For two months he dreaded that he might drown at any minute. For two months he thought of nothing but his father and his family.

Finally he arrived in a busy port city. He asked everywhere for his father, but no one in Chinatown had heard the name. There were thousands of Chinese flung throughout the New World, he was told. Gold miners scrabbled along icy rivers, farmers ploughed the long low valleys, and laborers traveled through towns and forests, from job to job. Who could find one single man in this enormous wilderness?

Young Chu was soon penniless. But he was young and strong, and he feared neither danger nor hard labor. He joined a work gang of thirty Chinese, and a steamer ferried them up a river canyon to build the railway.

When the morning mist lifted, Chu's mouth fell open. On both sides of the rushing river, gray mountains rose like walls to block the sky. The rock face dropped into ragged cliffs that only eagles could ascend and jutted out from cracks where scrawny trees clung. Never before had he seen such towering ranges of dark raw rock.

The crew pitched their tents and began to work. They hacked at hills with hand-scoops and shovels to level a pathway for the train. Their hammers and chisels chipped boulders into gravel and fill. Their dynamite and drills thrust tunnels deep into the mountain. At night, the crew would sit around the campfire chewing tobacco, playing cards and talking.

From one camp to another, the men trekked up the rail line, their food and tools dangling from sturdy shoulder poles. When they met other workers, Chu would run ahead and shout his father's name and ask for news. But the workers just shook their heads grimly.

"Search no more, young man!" one grizzled old worker said. "Don't you know that too many have died here? My own brother was buried alive in a mudslide."

"My uncle was killed in a dynamite blast," muttered another. "No one warned him about the fuse."

The angry memories rose and swirled like smoke among the workers.

"The white boss treats us like mules and dogs!"

"They need a railway to tie this nation together, but they can't afford to pay decent wages."

"What kind of country is this?"

Chu listened, but still he felt certain that his father was alive.

 Then winter came and halted all work. Snows buried everything under a heavy blanket of white. The white boss went to town to live in a warm hotel, but Chu and the workers stayed in camp. The men tied potato sacks around their feet and huddled by the fire, while ice storms howled like wolves through the mountains. Chu thought the winter would never end.

When spring finally arrived, the survivors struggled outside and shook the chill from their bones. They dug graves for two workers who had succumbed to sickness. They watched the river surge alive from the melting snow. Work resumed, and Chu began to search again for his father.

Late one afternoon, the gang reached a mountain with a half-finished tunnel. As usual, Chu ran up to shout his father's name, but before he could say a word, other workers came running out of the tunnel.

"It's haunted!" they cried. "Watch out! There are ghosts inside!"

"Dark figures slide soundlessly through the rocks!" one man whispered. "We hear heavy footsteps approaching but never arriving. We hear sighs and groans coming from corners where no man stands."

Chu's friends dropped their packs and refused to set up camp. But the white boss rode up on his horse and shook his fist at the men. "No work, no pay!" he shouted. "Now get to work!"

Then he galloped off. The workers squatted on the rocks and looked helplessly at one another. They needed the money badly for food and supplies.

Chu stood up. "What is there to fear?" he cried. "The ghosts have no reason to harm us. There is no reason to be afraid. We have hurt no one."

"Do you want to die?" a man called out.

"I will spend the night inside the tunnel," Chu declared as the men muttered unbelievingly. "Tomorrow we can work."

 Chu took his bedroll, a lamp, and food and marched into the mountain. He heard the crunch of his boots and water dripping. He knelt to light his lamp. Rocks lay in loose piles everywhere, and the shadowy walls closed in on him.

At the end of the tunnel he sat down and ate his food. He closed his eyes and wondered where his father was. He pictured his mother weeping in her bed and heard her voice calling his father's name. He lay down, pulled his blankets close, and eventually he fell asleep.

Chu awoke gasping for breath. Something heavy was pressing down on his chest. He tried to raise his arms but

could not. He clenched his fists and summoned all his strength, but still he was paralyzed. His eyes strained into the darkness, but saw nothing.

Suddenly the pressure eased and Chu groped for the lamp. As the chamber sprang into light, he cried, "What do you want? Who are you?"

Silence greeted him, and then a murmur sounded from behind. Chu spun around and saw a figure in the shadows. He slowly raised the lamp. The flickering light traveled up blood-stained trousers and a mud-encrusted jacket. Then Chu saw his father's face.

"Papa!" he whispered, lunging forward.

"No! Do not come closer!" The figure stopped him. "I am not of your world. Do not embrace me."

Tears rose in Chu's eyes. "So, it's true," he choked. "You . . . you have left us . . ."

His father's voice quivered with rage. "I am gone, but I am not done yet. My son, an accident here killed many men. A fuse exploded before the workers could run. A ton of rock dropped on us and crushed us flat. They buried the whites in a churchyard, but our bodies were thrown into the river, where the current swept us away. We have no final resting place."

Chu fell upon his knees. "What shall I do?"

His father's words filled the tunnel. "Take chopsticks; they shall be our bones. Take straw matting; that can be our flesh. Wrap them together and tie them tightly. Take the bundles to the mountain top high above the nests of eagles, and cover us with soil. Pour tea over our beds. Then we shall sleep in peace."

When Chu looked up, his father had vanished. He stumbled out of the tunnel and blurted the story to his friends. Immediately they prepared the bundles and sent him off with ropes and a shovel to the foot of the cliff, and Chu began to climb.

When he swung himself over the top of the cliff, he

was so high up that he thought he could see the distant ocean. He dug the graves deeper than any wild animal could dig, and laid the bundles gently in the earth.

Then Chu brought his fists together above his head and bowed three times. He knelt and touched his forehead to the soil three times. In a loud clear voice he declared, "Three times I bow, three things I vow. Your pain shall stop now, your sleep shall soothe you now, and I will never forget you. Farewell."

Then, hanging onto the rope looped around a tree, Chu slid slowly back down the cliff. When he reached the bottom, he looked back and saw that the rope had turned into a giant snake that was sliding smoothly up the rock face.

"Good," he smiled to himself. "It will guard the graves well." Then he returned to the camp, where he and his fellow workers lit their lamps and headed into the tunnel. And spirits never again disturbed them, nor the long trains that came later.

Our Chinese Spirits

by Paul Yee

When I was a child, my Aunt Lillian used to talk about ghosts. She claimed she had seen some and knew exactly how to identify them and what to do to keep them away. Listening to her, I remember swallowing the delicious thrill of wanting to hear more and more because getting scared was fun, but at the same time I dreaded her every word because then I'd be so afraid of the dark!

There's this old Chinese fear called "gwaih-jahk," which translates as "ghost-crush." Have you ever awakened suddenly in the middle of the night and found that your arms and legs are totally paralysed? And your eyes might be

Paul Yee and his older brother

wide open, but you can't move an inch? Well, the Chinese believe a ghost is lying on top, holding you down, crushing you.

Years later, a friend explained it. If you wake up suddenly from a deep sleep, your mind is awake, but your body muscles stay so relaxed that they won't respond to the brain. That's all it is. No ghosts hovering over you, no bogey man in your bedroom. But I still thought I'd use "ghost-crush" in my story.

My Aunt Lillian was born on the West Coast in 1895, and she grew up amidst many stories about the early Chinese. She wasn't a natural storyteller herself, but every now and then, she would pull out a snippet from the past. One that I remember, for no real reason, is, "When the Chinese were building the railway, it was so cold in the mountains they had to wrap potato sacks around their feet!"

And that was the whole story! I shrugged and didn't pay much attention. Of course, that line came back to me and came alive when I wrote "Spirits."

When I went to the university, I did a lot of research into the history of the Chinese in North America. I was particularly curious about building the railway because so many Chinese were killed in landslides, dynamite blasts, disease, and bad weather. Yet the few accounts of the Chinese working in the mountains came from newspapers, from travelers' letters, or from contractors' ledgers. I never found a story about railway building told by a Chinese. That was why I wanted to write "Spirits."

I made up the story. But I remember when I was small, traveling on the train and going through tunnels deep inside the mountains. And I remember being scared as the train chugged its way through the long darkness because it felt like the mountain had its own ghost stories to press into me.

Thinking About It

1. Does "Spirits of the Railway" bring comfort or fear? Why would it have been told by Chinese who came to America?

2. You have read three selections that are historical non-fiction and three that are historical fiction. What is similar and different about the two kinds of writing? Which do you like better? Why?

3. What might have happened after "Spirits of the Railway"? What happened to young Chu? What did he do? What would he tell his mother?

ANOTHER BOOK ABOUT THE RAILWAY

To American settlers, the railway meant progress. To the Chinese laborers, it meant hard work and abuse. To the Cheyenne, the locomotive meant invasion and death to themselves and to their way of life. Only once in American history did an Indian people wreck a train. *Death of the Iron Horse* by Paul Goble is the story of what happened on August 7, 1867.

On the Threshold of My Tongue

by Barry Lopez
★★★★ *From* Crow and Weasel ★★★★

 e careful and watch out for each other.
Remember that you are representing your
people as you travel," Mountain Lion
cautions Crow and Weasel as they prepare
to leave their families and their village. The
two young men have decided to travel
farther north than their people have ever
gone. Their fathers feel that this journey is
too dangerous, but Mountain Lion has seen Crow and
Weasel in his dream standing beside a wide river, and he
has persuaded the elders that the young men should go.

First they travel across the vast prairie and cross the
wide, fast-moving river they call Floating Ashes River.

They leave the known world of their people and soon en-
ter the dark and silently threatening northern forests.
Crow and Weasel's friendship and their newly-found
courage and strength help them through this time. As
they wander through a maze of lakes, they marvel over
caribou and moose and unusual birds.

Soon they reach a land where the sun barely sets be-
fore it rises again. Snow covers the ground when they
awake in the morning. Just as they are deciding to turn
back to the south, Weasel sees an unusual-looking people
coming toward them in skin boats. Thus they meet the
Inuit and stay awhile to share stories and experiences.
One day they realize they must hurry if they are to arrive
home before winter, so they say farewell to their new
friends and start their long journey south.

▶▶▶▶▶▶▶▶ ▶▶▶▶▶▶▶▶

 ROW and Weasel traveled south for half
the cycle of the moon. It was getting
colder, the Moon of Dry Grass at home,
but they traveled easily, riding with a
confident rhythm that was new to them,
which they noticed but did not remark
upon. They were flush with the knowledge of all that they had learned and seen.
It would get colder and they had a long way to go. But
they had covered this trail once before. And this time they
were drawn on by memories of what lay at the other end.

They found caribou more easily now when they were hungry. The horses seemed more sure-footed. Both the young mare and the colt were more alert, less skittish on the path.

Under cloudless skies the horses occasionally broke away at a full gallop. Crow and Weasel rode them south with a growing sense of the wonder of what they had done.

Half the cycle of the moon found them past the lake country, back on a path that bore their tracks. They rode for some days toward the forest. One evening before they stopped to camp they were hailed by someone in the fading light. They saw it was Badger when they rode up. She bid them enter her lodge, which was underground.

"I heard you coming toward me all day," said Badger with pleasure and excitement. "I hear everything, through the ground. Where have you come from?"

"We have been far to the north, but we live far away to the south and are headed home," said Crow.

"Well, you must stay here the night, and tell me of where you have been. There is good grass here for your horses, and no one around to bother them. We will have a good dinner and you will leave refreshed in the morning."

Crow and Weasel had never seen a lodge quite like Badger's. Quivers and parfleches, all beautifully decorated, hung from the walls, along with painted robes, birdbone breastplates, and many pieces of quillwork—leggings and moccasins, elktooth dresses, awl cases, and pipe bags. Lances decorated with strips of fur and small colored stones stood in the corners, and painted shields were hung on the walls beside medicine bundles. Other bundles were suspended from tripods.

 adger made up a good meal, and after they ate, Crow offered the pipe. In the silence that followed, Crow and Weasel felt a strange obligation to speak of what they had seen.

"Now tell me, my friends, what did you see up north? I have always wanted to know what it is like up there."

Weasel began to speak.

"My friend," said Badger. "Stand up, stand up here so you can express more fully what you have seen."

Weasel stood up, though he felt somewhat self-conscious in doing so. He began to speak about the people called Inuit and their habit of hunting an unusual white bear.

"Wait, my friend," said Badger. "Where were you when this happened?"

"We were in their camp. They told us."

"Well, tell me something about their camp."

Weasel described their camp, and then returned again to the story of hunting the bear.

"But, my friend," interrupted Badger, "tell me a little first of who these people are. What did they look like?"

Badger's words were beginning to annoy Weasel, but Crow could see what Badger was doing, and he smiled to himself. Weasel began again, but each time he would get only a little way in his story before Badger would ask for some point of clarification. Weasel was getting very irritated.

Finally Crow spoke up.

"Badger," he said, "my friend is trying very hard to tell his story. And I can see that you are only trying to help him, by teaching him to put the parts together in a good pattern, to speak with a pleasing rhythm, and to call on all the details of memory. But let us now see if he gets your meaning, for my friend is very smart."

"That is well put," said Badger, curious.

"Weasel," continued Crow, "do you remember what that man said before he began to tell us stories about Sedna and those other beings? He said, 'I have put my poem in order on the threshold of my tongue.' That's what this person Badger, who has taken us into her lodge, is saying. Pretend Badger and I are the people waiting back in our village. Speak to us with that kind of care."

Badger looked at Crow with admiration. Weasel, who had been standing uneasily before them, found his footing and his voice. He began to speak with a meas-ured, fetching rhythm, painting a picture of the country-side where they had been, and then drawing the Inuit people and the others, the caribou, up into life, drawing them up out of the ground.

hen Weasel finished, Badger nodded with gratitude, as though she had heard something profound.

"You know," she said to Weasel, "I have heard wondrous rumors of these Inuit people, but you are the first person I've heard tell a story about them who had himself been among them. You make me marvel at the strangeness of the world. That strangeness, the intriguing life of another people, it is a crucial thing, I think, to know."

"Now Crow," said Weasel, taking his seat, "tell Badger of our people and of our village. Tell her about this journey of ours."

Crow took his place in front of the other two. He also felt awkward, but with the help of Badger, a few pointed questions to sharpen his delivery, he began to speak strongly, with deliberation and care, about all that Weasel had asked him to say.

"You are fine young men," said Badger when Crow had finished. "I can see that. But you are beginning to sense your responsibilities, too, and the journey you have chosen is a hard one. If you keep going, one day you will be men. You will have families."

"We are very grateful for your hospitality, Badger," said Crow. "Each place we go, we learn something, and your wisdom here has helped us."

"I would ask you to remember only this one thing," said Badger. "The stories people tell have a way of taking

care of them. If stories come to you, care for them. And learn to give them away where they are needed. Sometimes a person needs a story more than food to stay alive. That is why we put these stories in each other's memory. This is how people care for themselves. One day you will be good storytellers. Never forget these obligations."

o one since Mountain Lion had spoken so directly to them of their obligations, but this time Crow and Weasel were not made uncomfortable. Each could understand what Badger was talking about, and each one knew that if his life went on he would one day know fully what Badger meant. For now, all it meant was that it was good to remember and to say well what happened, if someone asked to hear.

In the morning when they left, Badger told them a way to get through the forest that was not quite so difficult as the way they had come. "It is an open trail," she said, "and there are not so many trees. You will be able to go more quickly. But, still, it is a long way to your country. And soon it will be the first Snow Moon."

She gave them each a winter robe of buffalo. They gave her a beaded bag from home, which she accepted with wonder and humility. And they said goodbye.

Thinking About It

Crow and Weasel will create stories for the rest of their lives about their adventures this summer. What parts of their story would you like to hear more about?

What three key pieces of advice on telling his story does Crow give Weasel? What else would you need to know to be a good storyteller?

When Crow and Weasel arrive home, everyone asks about their adventures. Crow winks at Weasel and begins to tell the crowd about their encounter with Badger. What does Crow tell them?

A Time Never to Be Forgotten

★★★★ *by Doreen Rappaport* ★★★★

Maria Ascension Sepulveda y Avila led a comfortable life as the daughter of a wealthy cattle rancher. Ascension's grandparents were among the first Spanish settlers in the pueblo of Los Angeles in the 1780s and gradually acquired substantial land holdings. In 1837 Ascension's father added 48,000 acres to his grazing lands. Within ten years, with the influx of prospectors and settlers, he found a ready, lucrative market for his cattle, and made his fortune.

Ascension, the twelfth of thirteen children, was born in 1844. She spent most of her childhood with her oldest sister and her sister's husband, who lived in the family townhouse in Los Angeles. From age nine to sixteen she was sent to a convent school. When she was almost sixteen, she met her future husband, thirty-year-old Thomas Mott. Ascension describes her courtship and marriage to Mott in the well-chaperoned world of Spanish tradition.

 The first time I saw the man who was later to become my husband was when I was seven years old. My father had imported a fine race horse from Australia, the "Black Swan." The groom was accustomed to lead him around the corral for exercises, and frequently I was allowed to sit upon his back.

The gentlemen of the neighborhood used to come and watch the "Black Swan." One day came Mr. Thomas Mott. Even at that first sight of him I was impressed by his distinguished appearance.

He had come to San Francisco from New York in the year 1849 with the rush of gold seekers, making the journey by way of the Isthmus of Panama. In the year 1852 he came to Los Angeles and established himself in business.

The [third] time I saw Mr. Mott was just after I left the Convent in San Jose. I was barely sixteen and had been taken to my first ball by my sister. The only reason my sister took me was because there was no one at home with whom I could stay.

There were many guests, and I sat between my sister and my cousin. Dr. Winston, an old friend of the family, was standing near us and with him was a very handsome gentleman. They had been glancing in our direction for some time, so my cousin said, when finally they walked over and spoke to my sister and my cousin, apparently not noticing me at all. They exchanged a few remarks and then suddenly and to my extreme [embarrassment], Dr. Winston's friend, who was none other than Mr. Mott, leaned over and broke several handfuls of "cacarones" (confetti) on my head. The confetti was made from gilt paper and I was covered with the shimmering bits from the braids wound around my head to the hem of my ruffled white silk dress. Without a word Mr. Mott bowed and walked away. I was fresh from the Convent and I thought that the gentleman had very strange manners indeed.

Shortly after this incident Mr. Mott called upon my mother and father and told them that he would like to marry me and asked their permission to court me. My parents replied that I was very young but that he might call on me.

During his ensuing visits I never saw him alone. The room was always filled with members of my family and his remarks were chiefly addressed to them. My brother, Joaquin, was the only one of my brothers and sisters to favor Mr. Mott's suit. The others put as many obstacles in his way as possible.

I attended a ball at the Prudhomme home on one occasion and they surrounded me with people and arranged to have my dance program filled as quickly as possible so that Mr. Mott would be unable to obtain a dance with me. However, his good friend, Dr. Winston, gave him his dance with me, and presently Mr. Mott walked over to me and asked if I would grant him the favor of a dance. I replied that I was sorry but I was afraid I had none left and then he explained Dr. Winston's kindness.

Whenever Mr. Mott called to take me riding I was always accompanied by some of my women relations, one of whom sat in the front seat with him. On one occasion, just as my sister, Francisca, was about to occupy the front seat as usual, my kind cousin Josefa pulled her back and insisted on my being permitted to sit with Mr. Mott. I was forbidden however to speak any English as they could not understand it, and as Mr. Mott spoke little Spanish it can be readily imagined that the conversation lagged somewhat. However, he managed to write a little poem on a scrap of paper and hand it to me surreptitiously. I tucked it away in my dress and later read it in the privacy of my boudoir. I still have the paper to this day.

Shortly after this Mr. Mott asked if he might see me alone to ask for my hand in marriage. It was willingly granted as they thought from my assumed indifference that I would refuse him. I did refuse him this time telling him that I was too young and that I was not going to think of marriage for a while. I was very touched by his unhappiness when he left me and gave him a flower from the garden.

He went to Santa Barbara soon after and those who were opposed to the match saw to it that rumors reached my ears that [he] was paying a great deal of attention to certain other young ladies, which of course did not add to my happiness.

Pio Pico was a good friend of ours, and Mr. Mott finally enlisted his aid. It happened that the Carlisles' first son was to be christened and Mr. Pico arranged that Mr. Mott should call to ask me to be godmother. There were many guests at the ceremony and when Mr. Mott and I arrived the Priest, Father Blas Rho, called out to us before them all and asked if we wished him to marry us.

Soon after this Mr. Mott presented an engagement ring to my father and mother and they placed it upon my finger. Mr. Mott then left for San Francisco. I did not even kiss him good-bye as I did not consider it proper until after I should become his wife.

In the meantime, women from Sonora came down to the ranch to sew my trousseau. My lingerie was made of linen and trimmed with drawn-work. My dresses and the rest of my things came from San Francisco.

Mr. Mott came down from San Francisco in time to attend a ball given in our honor on the 8th of December at the Bella Union. I had been down on the ranch over-

seeing the making of my trousseau, and rode the whole distance of thirty-five miles back to town on horseback in the pouring rain. When I arrived home, I was too utterly exhausted to attend the ball, which proceeded to be given without its guest of honor.

I was married at eight o'clock in the evening on December 23, 1861, at the home of my parents. My father had sent to Santa Barbara for the musicians, eight in number. The wonderful cakes and other things for the supper which followed the ceremony were all brought from San Francisco. Lanterns were strung all about the grounds giving a very gay effect.

My wedding gown was of white silk made with three flounces which were bordered with blocks of satin. The veil was of Alençon lace, and my wreath and bouquet were of artificial flowers.

My attendants were my cousin and Mrs. Carlisle. [One wore a gown] of white silk made with three flounces of lace embroidered in colors; [the other's] gown was of wine colored velvet.

We were married by Father Blas Rho.

Immediately after the supper we all went over to the Bella Union Hotel for the ball which was given us by Mr. Mott's friends. It was a very gay occasion. The guests were many and from all parts of California. At one time eighty couples were dancing the contra-dance.

My husband and I remained at the Hotel after the ball. The wedding guests from out of town were obliged to remain for six weeks as it rained without stopping the better part of that time, and the country was so flooded that it was impossible to reach San Pedro whence the steamer sailed once a month. My father's house was overflowing with guests and as the musicians were among those detained by the floods, the better part of the time was spent in dancing and gaiety. It was a time never to be forgotten.

Being a Detective

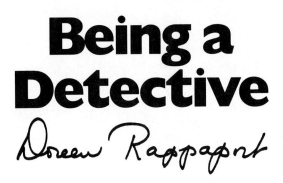

by Doreen Rappaport

Being a historian is like being a detective. Detectives follow up clues or fragments of clues. They question witnesses and visit places where the person has been. Sometimes a clue that looks really good leads nowhere. Then the detective patiently reviews the remaining evidence and tries to figure out what to do next.

When I decided to create a documentary history of the lives of women in the United States, I wanted to include a memoir by a Hispanic woman in the West, for the Spanish were the first European settlers in the Southwest and the West. I knew finding this memoir would be difficult, because until recently historians haven't paid too much attention to Hispanic women.

I telephoned a few historians who specialize in Hispanic American history. They generously shared their knowledge, but unfortunately I don't read Spanish and much of the material they suggested was written in Spanish. I telephoned libraries with important archives about the West. The archivists told me I would have to come there and dig out the documents myself.

I went back to New York City's Research Library at 42nd Street. A librarian referred me to a bibliography that was only about women. In the section on life in the West, I carefully read through the names of hundreds of articles and manuscripts on women, until I came across an article in a history journal about a 19th century Hispanic woman in California. I raced to the magazine index, marked down the library number, and put in a request for the journal.

I wasn't disappointed. The article contained excerpts from a lively account of the courtship and wedding of Maria Ascension Sepulveda y Avila. In a footnote to the article, the historian thanked Ascension's great-granddaughter who had lent her the memoir.

But where did the great-granddaughter live? In California? And where in California? How would I find her? I did two things at once. I wrote a letter, in care of the history journal, to the author of the article asking her if she would be kind enough to send me the woman's address and phone number. Then I called California telephone information until an operator tracked down a last name that matched the name of the great-granddaughter. My hands were shaking as I dialed the number. Had I found the great-granddaughter? Would she allow me to reprint the memoir in my book?

You know the answer to this mystery.

Thinking About It

★★★★

1 You have Ascension's own words. Through those words, you can look into her memories. What do you think of her as you read her words? Were her problems in any way similar to yours?

2 Diaries, journals, and autobiographies are of interest to find out about the past. What do you find in Ascension's memoir that makes it helpful or enjoyable? Give examples and explain.

3 What would you report as "a time never to be forgotten" in your own life, to be found and wondered at 150 years from now?

The New Colossus

by Emma Lazarus

Not like the brazen giant of Greek fame,
With conquering limbs astride from land to land;
Here at our sea-washed, sunset gates shall stand
A mighty woman with a torch, whose flame
Is the imprisoned lightning, and her name
Mother of Exiles. From her beacon-hand
Glows world-wide welcome; her mild eyes command
The air-bridged harbor that twin cities frame.

"Keep, ancient lands, your storied pomp!" cries she
With silent lips. "Give me your tired, your poor,
Your huddled masses yearning to breathe free,
The wretched refuse of your teeming shore.
Send these, the homeless, tempest-tost to me,
I lift my lamp beside the golden door!"

I Hear America Singing

by Walt Whitman

I hear America singing, the varied carols I hear;
Those of mechanics—each one singing his, as it should
    be, blithe and strong;
The carpenter singing his, as he measures his plank
    or beam,
The mason singing his, as he makes ready for work, or
    leaves off work;
The boatman singing what belongs to him in his boat—
    the deckhand singing on the steamboat deck;
The shoemaker singing as he sits on his bench—the hat-
    ter singing as he stands;
The wood-cutter's song—the ploughboy's, on his way
    in the morning, or at the noon intermission, or
    at sundown;
The delicious singing of the mother—or of the young
    wife at work—or of the girl sewing or washing—
    Each singing what belongs to her, and to none else;
The day what belongs to the day—At night, the party of
    young fellows, robust, friendly,
Singing, with open mouths, their strong melodious songs.

Initiation to America

★★★★ *by Mary Antin* ★★★★

Our initiation into American ways began with the first step on the new soil. My father found occasion to instruct or correct us even on the way from the pier to Wall Street, which journey we made crowded together in a rickety cab. He told us not to lean out of the windows, not to point, and explained the word "greenhorn." We did not want to be "greenhorns," and gave the strictest attention to my father's instructions. I do not know when my parents found opportunity to review together the history of Polotsk in the three years past, for we children had no patience with the subject; my mother's narrative was constantly interrupted by irrelevant questions, interjections, and explanations.

The first meal was an object lesson of much variety. My father produced several kinds of food, ready to eat, without any cooking, from little tin cans that had printing all over them. He attempted to introduce us to a queer, slippery kind of fruit, which he called "banana," but had to give it up for the time being. After the meal, he had better luck with a curious piece of furniture on runners, which he called "rocking-chair." There were five of us newcomers, and we found five different ways of getting into the American machine of perpetual motion, and as many ways of getting out of it. One born and bred to the use of a rocking-chair cannot imagine how ludicrous people can make themselves when attempting to use it for the first time. We laughed immoderately over our various experiments with the novelty, which was a wholesome way of letting off steam after the unusual excitement of the day.

In our flat we did not think of such a thing as storing the coal in the bathtub. There was no bathtub. So in the evening of the first day my father conducted us to the public baths. As we moved along in a little procession, I was delighted with the illumination of the streets. So many lamps, and they burned until morning, my father said, and so people did not need to carry lanterns. In America, then, everything was free, as we had heard in Russia. Light was free; the streets were as bright as a synagogue on a holy day. Music was free; we had been serenaded, to our gaping delight, by a brass band of many pieces, soon after our installation on Union Place.

Education was free. That subject my father had written about repeatedly, as comprising his chief hope for us children, the essence of American opportunity, the treasure that no thief could touch, not even misfortune or poverty. It was the one thing that he was able to promise us when he sent for us; surer, safer than bread or shelter. On our second day I was thrilled with the realization of what this freedom of education meant. A little girl from across the alley came and offered to conduct us to school. My father was out, but we five between us had a few words of English by this time. We knew the word school.

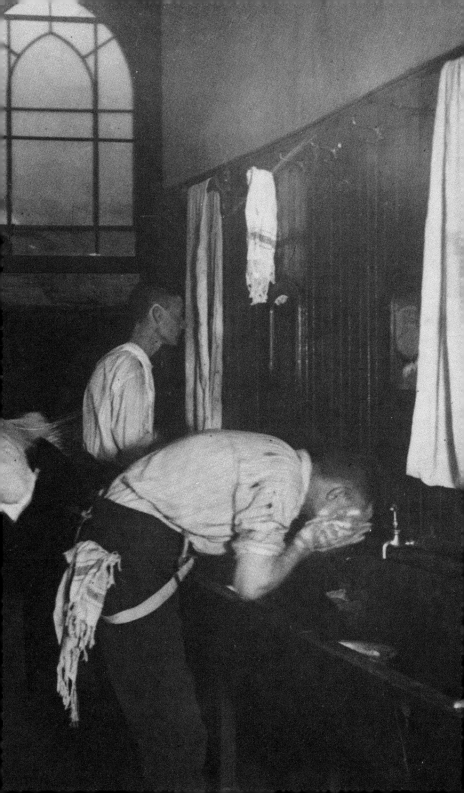

We understood. This child who had never seen us till yesterday, who could not pronounce our names, who was not much better dressed than we, was able to offer us the freedom of the schools of Boston! No application made; no questions asked; no examinations, rulings, exclusions; no machinations; no fees. The doors stood open for every one of us. The smallest child could show us the way.

This incident impressed me more than anything I had heard in advance of the freedom of education in America. It was concrete proof—almost the thing itself. One had to experience it to understand it.

Father himself conducted us to school. He would not have delegated that mission to the President of the United States. He had awaited the day with impatience equal to mine, and the visions he saw as he hurried us over the sun-flecked pavements transcended all my dreams. Almost his first act on landing on American soil, three years before, had been his application for naturalization. He had taken the remaining steps in the process with eager promptness, and at the earliest moment allowed by the law, he became a citizen of the United States. It is true that he had left home in search of bread for his hungry family, but he went blessing the necessity that drove him to America. The boasted freedom of the New World meant to him far more than the right to reside, travel, and work wherever he pleased; it meant the freedom to speak his thoughts, to throw off the shackles of superstition, to test his own fate, unhindered by political or religious tyranny. He was only a young man when he landed—thirty-two; and most of his life he had been held in leading-strings. He was hungry for his untasted manhood. . . .

At last the four of us stood around the teacher's desk; and my father, in his impossible English, gave us over in her charge, with some broken word of his hopes for us that his swelling heart could no longer contain. I venture

to say that Miss Nixon was struck by something uncommon in the group we made, something outside of Semitic features and the abashed manner of the alien. My little sister was as pretty as a doll, with her clear pink-and-white face, short golden curls, and eyes like blue violets when you caught them looking up. My brother might have been a girl, too, with his cherubic contours of face, rich red color, glossy black hair, and fine eyebrows. Whatever secret fears were in his heart, remembering his former teachers, who had taught with the rod, he stood up straight and uncringing before the American teacher, his cap respectfully doffed. Next to him stood a starved-looking girl with eyes ready to pop out, and short dark curls that would not have made much of a wig for a Jewish bride.

 All three children carried themselves rather better than the common run of "green" pupils that were brought to Miss Nixon. But the figure that challenged attention to the group was the tall, straight father, with his earnest face and fine forehead, nervous hands eloquent in gesture, and a voice full of feeling. This foreigner, who brought his children to school as if it were an act of consecration, who regarded the teacher of the primer class with reverence, who spoke of visions, like a man inspired, in a common schoolroom, was not like other aliens, who brought their children in dull obedience to the law; was not like the native fathers, who brought their unmanageable boys, glad to be relieved of their care. I think Miss Nixon guessed what my father's best English could not convey. I think she divined that by the simple act of delivering our school certificates to her he took possession of America.

Thinking About It

1. Mary Antin's real-life initiation to America seems filled with pleasant memories. How does she share them with you? What do you think of her as you read them?

2. What is Mary talking about when she says that in America, "everything is free"? Are those things still free today? What things are still "free" today?

3. Everyone has been initiated into something: an experience that required facing new and strange things. When have you had such an experience? How did you react? How can you communicate that experience to others?

ANOTHER BOOK ABOUT NEW EXPERIENCES
Drew Ralston loves America as much as Mary does, but growing up a farmer's son in Kansas in 1934 is tough. In *Moxie* by Phyllis Rossiter, the winds carry off the farm bit by bit and the relentless sun bakes the land. What should be a wonderful summer after graduation forces Drew to become a teenager and man at the same time.

I Have a Dream

by Martin Luther King, Jr.

 say to you, my friends, that even though we must face the difficulties of today and tomorrow, I still have a dream. It is a dream deeply rooted in the American dream that one day this nation will rise up and live out the true meaning of its creed— we hold these truths to be self-evident, that all men are created equal.

I have a dream that one day on the red hills of Georgia, sons of former slaves and sons of former slave-owners will be able to sit down together at the table of brotherhood.

I have a dream that one day, even the state of Mississippi, a state sweltering with the heat of injustice, sweltering with the heat of oppression, will be transformed into an oasis of freedom and justice.

I have a dream my four little children will one day live in a nation where they will not be judged by the color of their skin but by content of their character. I have a dream today!

I have a dream that one day, down in Alabama, with its vicious racists, with its governor having his lips dripping with the words of interposition and nullification, that one day, right there in Alabama, little black boys and black girls will be able to join hands with little white

boys and white girls as sisters and brothers. I have a dream today!

I have a dream that one day every valley shall be exalted, every hill and mountain shall be made low, the rough places shall be made plain, and the crooked places shall be made straight and the glory of the Lord will be revealed and all flesh shall see it together.

This is our hope. This is the faith that I go back to the South with.

With this faith we will be able to hew out of the mountain of despair a stone of hope. With this faith we will be able to transform the jangling discords of our nation into a beautiful symphony of brotherhood.

With this faith we will be able to work together, to pray together, to struggle together, to go to jail together, to stand up for freedom together, knowing that we will be free one day. This will be the day when all of God's children will be able to sing with new meaning—"my country 'tis of thee; sweet land of liberty; of thee I sing; land where my fathers died, land of the pilgrim's pride; from every mountain side, let freedom ring"—and if America is to be a great nation, this must become true.

So let freedom ring from the prodigious hilltops of New Hampshire.

Let freedom ring from the mighty mountains of New York.

Let freedom ring from the heightening Alleghenies of Pennsylvania.

Let freedom ring from the snow-capped Rockies of Colorado.

Let freedom ring from the curvaceous slopes of California.

But not only that.

Let freedom ring from Stone Mountain of Georgia.

Let freedom ring from Lookout Mountain of Tennessee.

Let freedom ring from every hill and molehill of Mississippi, from every mountainside, let freedom ring.

And when we allow freedom to ring, when we let it ring from every village and hamlet, from every state and city, we will be able to speed up that day when all of God's children—black men and white men, Jews and Gentiles, Catholics and Protestants—will be able to join hands and to sing in the words of the old Negro spiritual, "Free at last, free at last; thank God Almighty, we are free at last."

THINKING ABOUT IT

1 Martin Luther King, Jr., gave this speech in 1963. As you read it, listen to hear his voice in his words. What in the speech—in its words and in the way he must have said them— is still important and relevant today?

2 Dr. King uses the same phrase to begin many sentences. What is that phrase? Why did he use this repetition?

3 *You* have a dream! What is your vision of how America should be?

from

The People, Yes

by Carl Sandburg

They have yarns
   Of a skyscraper so tall they had to put hinges
   On the two top stories so to let the moon go by,
   Of one corn crop in Missouri when the roots
   Went so deep and drew off so much water
   The Mississippi river bed that year was dry,
   Of pancakes so thin they had only one side,
Of "a fog so thick we shingled the barn and six feet out
   on the fog,"
Of Pecos Pete straddling a cyclone in Texas and riding it
   to the west coast where "it rained out under him,"

Of the man who drove a swarm of bees across the
Rocky Mountains and the Desert "and didn't lose
a bee,"
Of a mountain railroad curve where the engineer in his
cab can touch the caboose and spit in the
conductor's eye,
Of the boy who climbed a cornstalk growing so fast he
would have starved to death if they hadn't shot
biscuits up to him,
Of the old man's whiskers: "When the wind was with
him his whiskers arrived a day before he did,"
Of the hen laying a square egg and cackling, "Ouch!"
and of hens laying eggs with the dates printed
on them,
Of the ship captain's shadow: it froze to the deck one
cold winter night,
Of mutineers on that same ship put to chipping rust
with rubber hammers,
Of the sheep counter who was fast and accurate: "I just
count their feet and divide by four,"
Of the man so tall he must climb a ladder to
shave himself,
Of the runt so teeny-weeny it takes two men and a boy
to see him,
Of mosquitoes: one can kill a dog, two of them a man,
Of a cyclone that sucked cookstoves out of the kitchen,
up the chimney flue, and on to the next town,
Of the same cyclone picking up wagon-tracks in
Nebraska and dropping them over in the Dakotas,
Of the hook-and-eye snake unlocking itself into forty
pieces, each piece two inches long, then in nine
seconds flat snapping itself together again,
Of the watch swallowed by the cow—when they
butchered her a year later the watch was running
and had the correct time,

Of horned snakes, hoop snakes that roll themselves
      where they want to go, and rattlesnakes carrying
      bells instead of rattles on their tails,
Of the herd of cattle in California getting lost in a giant
      redwood tree that had hollowed out,
Of the man who killed a snake by putting its tail in its
      mouth so it swallowed itself,
Of railroad trains whizzing along so fast they reach the
      station before the whistle,
Of pigs so thin the farmer had to tie knots in their tails
      to keep them from crawling through the cracks in
      their pens,
Of Paul Bunyan's big blue ox, Babe, measuring between
      the eyes forty-two ax-handles and a plug of Star
      tobacco exactly,
Of John Henry's hammer and the curve of its swing and
      his singing of it as "a rainbow round my shoulder."

"Do tell!"
"I want to know!"

The Vision of
Maya Ying Lin

by Brent Ashabranner

The Vietnam Memorial had been authorized by Congress "in honor and recognition of the men and women of the Armed Forces of the United States who served in the Vietnam War." The law, however, said not a word about what the memorial should be or what it should look like. That was left up to the Vietnam Veterans Memorial Fund, but the law did state that the memorial design and plans would have to be approved by the Secretary of the Interior, the Commission of Fine Arts, and the National Capital Planning Commission.

What would the memorial be? What should it

look like? Who would design it? Scruggs, Doubek, and Wheeler[1] didn't know, but they were determined that the memorial should help bring closer together a nation still bitterly divided by the Vietnam War. It couldn't be something like the Marine Corps Memorial showing American troops planting a flag on enemy soil at Iwo Jima. It couldn't be a giant dove with an olive branch of peace in its beak. It had to soothe passions, not stir them up. But there was one thing Jan Scruggs insisted on: the memorial, whatever it turned out to be, would have to show the name of every man and woman killed or missing in the war.

The answer, they decided, was to hold a national design competition open to all Americans. The winning design would receive a prize of $20,000, but the real prize would be the winner's knowledge that the memorial would become a part of American history on the Mall in Washington, D.C. Although fund raising was only well started at this point, the choosing of a memorial design could not be delayed if the memorial was to be built by Veterans Day, 1982.

H. Ross Perot contributed the $160,000 necessary to hold the competition, and a panel of distinguished architects, landscape architects, sculptors, and design specialists was chosen to decide the winner.

Announcement of the competition in October, 1980, brought an astonishing response. The Vietnam Veterans Memorial Fund received over five thousand inquiries. They came from every state in the nation and from every field of design; as ex-

---

[1]Jan Scruggs, Robert Doubek, and John Wheeler were three Vietnam veterans who headed the Vietnam Veterans Memorial Fund and worked hard to make the memorial a reality.

pected, architects and sculptors were particularly interested. Everyone who inquired received a booklet explaining the criteria. Among the most important: the memorial could not make a political statement about the war; it must contain the names of all persons killed or missing in action in the war; it must be in harmony with its location on the Mall.

total of 2,573 individuals and teams registered for the competition. They were sent photographs of the memorial site, maps of the area around the site and of the entire Mall, and other technical design information. The competitors had three months to prepare their designs, which had to be received by March 31, 1981.

Of the 2,573 registrants, 1,421 submitted designs, a record number for such a design competition. When the designs were spread out for jury selection, they filled a large airplane hangar. The jury's task was to select the design which, in their judgment, was the best in meeting these criteria:

- *a design that honored the memory of those Americans who served and died in the Vietnam War.*
- *a design of high artistic merit.*
- *a design which would be harmonious with its site, including visual harmony with the Lincoln Memorial and the Washington Monument.*
- *a design that could take its place in the "historic continuity" of America's national art.*
- *a design that would be buildable, durable, and not too hard to maintain.*

The designs were displayed without any indication of the designer's name so that they could be judged anonymously, on their design merits alone. The jury spent one week reviewing all the designs in the airplane hangar. On May 1 it made its report to the Vietnam Veterans Memorial Fund; the experts declared Entry Number 1,026 the winner. The report called it "the finest and most appropriate" of all submitted and said it was "superbly harmonious" with the site on the Mall. Remarking upon the "simple and forthright" materials needed to build the winning entry, the report concludes:

This memorial with its wall of names, becomes a place of quiet reflection, and a tribute to those who served their nation in difficult times. All who come here can find it a place of healing. This will be a quiet memorial, one that achieves an excellent relationship with both the Lincoln Memorial and Washington Monument, and relates the visitor to them. It is uniquely horizontal, entering the earth rather than piercing the sky.

This is very much a memorial of our own times, one that could not have been achieved in another time and place. The designer has created an eloquent place where the simple meeting of earth, sky and remembered names contain messages for all who will know this place.

The eight jurors signed their names to the report, a unanimous decision. When the name of the winner was revealed, the art and architecture worlds were stunned. It was not the name of a nationally famous architect or sculptor, as most people had been sure it would be. The creator of Entry Number 1,026 was a twenty-one-year-old student at Yale University. Her name—unknown as yet in any field of art or architecture—was Maya Ying Lin.

How could this be?

How could an undergraduate student win one of the most important design competitions ever held? How could she beat out some of the top names in American art and architecture? Who was Maya Ying Lin?

The answer to that question provided some of the other answers, at least in part. Maya Lin, reporters soon discovered, was a Chinese American girl who had been born and raised in the small midwestern city of Athens, Ohio. Her father, Henry Huan Lin, was a ceramicist of considerable reputation and dean of fine arts at Ohio University in Athens. Her mother, Julia C. Lin, was a poet and professor of Oriental and English literature. Maya Lin's parents were born to culturally prominent families in China. When the Communists came to power in China in the 1940s, Henry and Julia Lin left the country and in time made their way to the United States.

Maya Lin grew up in an environment of art and literature. She was interested in sculpture and made both small and

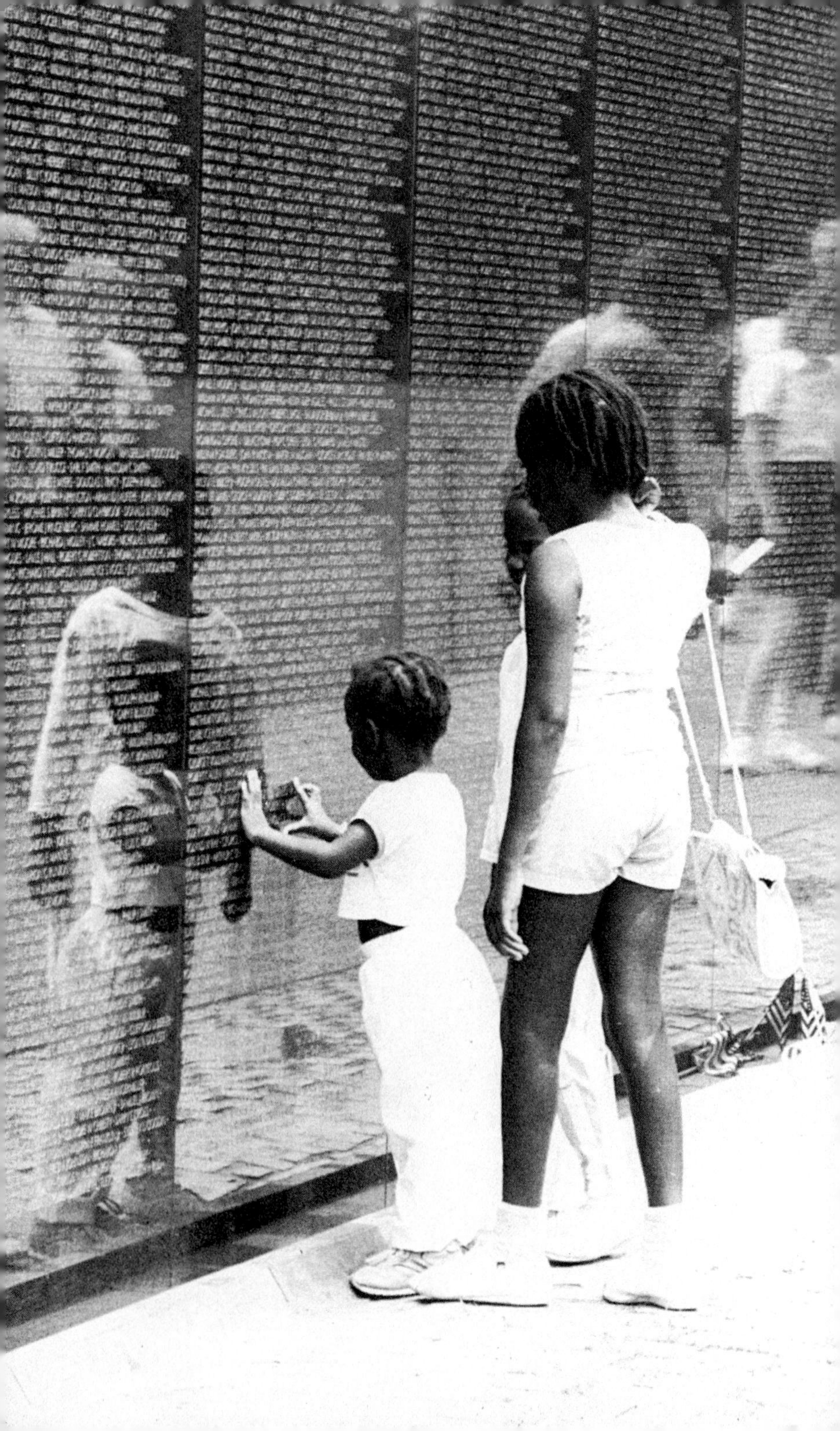

large sculptural figures, one cast in bronze. She learned silversmithing and made jewelry. She was surrounded by books and read a great deal, especially fantasies such as *The Hobbit* and *Lord of the Rings*.

But she also found time to work at McDonald's. "It was about the only way to make money in the summer," she said.

A covaledictorian at high school graduation, Maya Lin went to Yale without a clear notion of what she wanted to study and eventually decided to major in Yale's undergraduate program in architecture. During her junior year she studied in Europe and found herself increasingly interested in cemetery architecture. "In Europe there's very little space, so graveyards are used as parks," she said. "Cemeteries are cities of the dead in European countries, but they are also living gardens."

In France, Maya Lin was deeply moved by the war memorial to those who died in the Somme offensive in 1916 during World War I. The great arch by architect Sir Edwin Lutyens is considered one of the world's most outstanding war memorials.

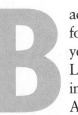

Back at Yale for her senior year, Maya Lin enrolled in Professor Andrus Burr's course in funerary (burial) architecture. The Vietnam Veterans Memorial competition had recently been announced, and although the memorial would be a cenotaph—a monument in honor of persons buried someplace else—Professor Burr thought that having his students prepare a design of the memorial would be a worthwhile course assignment.

Surely, no classroom exercise ever had such spectacular results.

After receiving the assignment, Maya Lin and two of her classmates decided to make the day's journey from New Haven, Connecticut, to Washington to look at the site where the memorial would be built. On the day of their visit, Maya Lin remembers, Constitution Gardens was awash with a late November sun; the park was full of light, alive with joggers and people walking beside the lake.

t was while I was at the site that I designed it," Maya Lin said later in an interview about the memorial with *Washington Post* writer Phil McCombs. "I just sort of visualized it. It just popped into my head. Some people were playing Frisbee. It was a beautiful park. I didn't want to destroy a living park. You use the landscape. You don't fight with it. You absorb the landscape . . . When I looked at the site I just knew I wanted something hori-zontal that took you in, that made you feel safe within the park, yet at the same time reminding you of the dead. So I just imagined opening up the earth. . . ."

When Maya Lin returned to Yale, she made a clay model of the vision that had come to her in Constitution Gardens. She showed it to Professor Burr; he liked her conception and encouraged her to enter the memorial competition. She put her design on paper, a task that took six weeks, and mailed it to Washington barely in time to meet the March 31 deadline.

A month and a day later, Maya Lin was attending class. Her roommate slipped into the classroom and handed her a note. Washington was calling and would call back in fifteen minutes. Maya Lin hurried to her room. The call came. She had won the memorial competition.

Pulling It All Together

1 What lesson can you learn from Maya Ying Lin's success? How can you apply it to your own life?

2 Whom would you nominate from this book for "Citizen for the Ages," an award for someone who has made a lasting public or private contribution to the nation? Build your case.

3 Design a monument to the characters, fictitious and nonfictitious, who form the spirit of this book. Your monument should be what you want it to be: visual, verbal, or another choice.

ANOTHER BOOK ABOUT VISIONS

On the lighter side, Paul and Sheldon have a vision of the ideal high school, but *Don't Care High* (by Gordon Korman)—excuse me!—Don Carey High School is not an example of a great educational institution. Paul and Sheldon turn the school around—if you call nearly inciting a riot at a science fair or bringing down the house at a basketball game, turning the school around!

Books to Enjoy

The Fighting Ground
by Avi
Harper, 1984
It is 1778 and Jonathan is helping his father on the farm
when they hear alarm bells from the nearby town. Without letting his parents know, Jonathan joins with some
neighbors and marches off to fight the British. One
surprise follows another as Jonathan learns about war.

Let the Hurricane Roar
by Rose Wilder Lane
Harper, 1961
Newlyweds Molly and David are only sixteen and
eighteen years old when they head west to find a
homestead. With no money, only the bare necessities
of supplies, a baby on the way, and winter approaching—will they survive?

The Chinese Americans
by Milton Meltzer
Crowell, 1980
Their dreams burst right away: America was not the
land of peace and plenty. The first Chinese to emi-
grate found low wages, ridicule, abuse, and violence.
Though they made great contributions to the pioneer
West, their efforts went unrecognized. But in the
course of time, their trials became triumphs as

Chinese Americans took their rightful place in
American culture and society.

Heartland
by Diane Siebert
Paintings by Wendell Minor
Crowell, 1989
Poetry and painting weave a marvelous tapestry cele-
brating America's heartland, the Midwest.

The Private War of Lillian Adams
by Barbara Corcoran
Atheneum, 1989
Lillian was caught in two wars: World War I in Europe
and an espionage war at home. With spies on her mind,
Lillian plays her own war games, only to find out some
unexpected truths.

A Long, Hard Journey: The Story of the Pullman Porter
by Patricia and Frederick McKissack
Walker & Co., 1989
Soon after the Civil War, the Pullman sleeping car was
designed so that people making long train trips could ride
in luxury. These cars were staffed with emancipated
slaves, proud to be working and to be making passengers
happy and comfortable. Descriptions and many photographs show the luxury of the Pullman cars and the hard
work of the porters. Seventy years later, however, a new
generation of porters realized they were working long
hours for low wages, and so the first black-controlled
union fought a David-and-Goliath battle against the
Pullman Company.

Literary Terms

Exaggeration Exaggeration is a way of writing humorously by making statements so outrageous they could not possibly be true. "The People, Yes" is a collection of such exaggerated statements that are a part of American folklore.

Historical Fiction Historical fiction is realistic fiction set in the past. It is a combination of fact and fiction, using real or fictional characters in a factually accurate setting to act out a fictional plot. "Meeting Uncle Jed" has fictional character Will meet his Uncle Jed just after the Civil War. "Spirits of the Railway" has fictional young Chu leave his home in China to seek his father in America.

Historical Nonfiction Historical nonfiction tells about real people and events from the past. Historical nonfiction may tell of an event or a series of events in a historical period. When it is told in a storylike form, it is called narrative nonfiction. "So I Became a Soldier" is an example of narrative historical nonfiction. Expository nonfiction is written to give information about an object, idea, theme, or event. "Expedition to the Pacific" is an example of expository historical nonfiction.

Primary Source Primary sources are original materials from a particular historical period. These might be accounts written by people who actually observed or participated in the events they described. **Primary sources** might be in the form of documents, letters, diaries, speeches, or songs from the period. The "I Have a Dream" speech is an example of a **primary source.**

Repetition   **Repetition** enhances the language and shapes the experience an audience has with a piece of writing. "The People, Yes" is a poem that uses **repetition.** The repeated pattern of the word "of" at the beginning of each line highlights all the wonderful tall tales told by American settlers and adds richness to the poem. Martin Luther King, Jr., used **repetition** effectively at the end of "I Have a Dream," repeating the phrase "let freedom ring" ten times.

Sonnet   A **sonnet** is a 14-line poem, often made up of an eight-line section followed by a six-line section that resolves the theme. "The New Colossus" is a **sonnet.** The first eight lines have one rhyme scheme; the last six lines have another. The last lines underscore what the Statue of Liberty represents.

Speech   A **speech** is a form of writing for oral delivery. Some **speeches** are similar to essays, for the speaker takes a stand on a topic and argues his case. "I Have a Dream" is Martin Luther King, Jr.'s, strongly worded plea for freedom for all people.

Glossary

Vocabulary from your selections

ag gra vate (ag′rə vāt), *v.t.,* **-vat ed, -vat ing.**
1 make more burdensome; make worse; exacerbate: *The danger from foreign enemies was aggravated by rebellion at home.* 2 make more serious or offensive: *A lie will only aggravate your guilt.* 3 INFORMAL. annoy; irritate; exasperate.

ap praise (ə prāz′), *v.t.,* **-praised, -prais ing.**
1 estimate the quality or merit of; judge: *Few can properly appraise the work of a new artist.* 2 estimate the value of; fix a price for; value: *The paintings were appraised at $100,000.*

ban (ban), *v.,* **banned, ban ning.** 1 forbid by law or authority; prohibit: *Swimming is banned in this lake.* 2 place a ban on; pronounce a curse on.

blurt (blėrt), *v.t.* Usually, **blurt out,** say suddenly or thoughtlessly: *blurt out the secret.*

board (bôrd, bōrd), *n.* 1 a broad, thin piece of wood for use in building, etc. 2 a flat piece of wood or other material used for some special purpose, as for drawing on, posting notices, etc. 3 tablet or frame on which pieces are moved in some games: *a backgammon board.* 4 pasteboard: *a book with covers of board.* 5 either of the rectangular pieces of strong pasteboard, used to make the hard covers of a book. 6 table to serve food on; table. 7 food served on a table, especially meals provided for pay at a boardinghouse, etc.

brood (brüd), *v.i.* 1 (of birds) sit on eggs so as to hatch them; incubate. 2 cover or protect young with or as if with the wings. 3 think or worry a long time about some one thing. 4 **brood on** or **brood over, a** keep thinking about. **b** hover over; hang close over.

broth er hood (bruŦH′ər hùd), *n.* 1 bond between brothers; feeling of brother for brother. 2 association of men with some common aim, characteristic, belief, profession, etc. 3 members of such an association; persons joined as brothers.

cav al ry (kav′əl rē), *n., pl.* **-ries.** 1 (formerly) soldiers who fought on horseback. 2 branch of an army in which soldiers fought on horseback, now modernized and equipped with armored vehicles, especially tanks.

con se crate (kon′sə krāt), v., -crat ed, -crat ing.
—v.t. **1** set apart as sacred; make holy; sanctify:
*The new chapel in the church was consecrated
by the bishop.* **2** make an object of veneration or
cherished regard; hallow: *Time has consecrated
these customs.*

con se cra tion (kon′sə krā′shən), n. **1** a conse-
crating. **2** a being consecrated. **3** ordination to a
sacred office, especially to that of bishop.

con ti nu i ty (kon′tə nü′ə tē, kon′tə nyü′ə tē), n.,
pl. **-ties. 1** condition or quality of being continuous. **2** a continuous or connected whole; uninterrupted succession; unbroken series.

con tin u ous (kən tin′yü əs), adj. without a stop
or break; connected; unbroken; uninterrupted: *a
continuous line, a continuous sound.*

cour te ous (kėr′tē əs), adj. thoughtful of others;
polite; civil.

cow ard (kou′ərd), n. person who lacks courage or
is easily made afraid; person who runs from
danger, trouble, etc. —adj. lacking courage;
cowardly. [< Old French *coart* < *coe* tail < Latin
coda, cauda; with reference to an animal with its
tail between its legs]

cra dle board (krā′dl bôrd, krā′dl bōrd), n. a
board or flat framework to which American
Indians traditionally bound a child during infan-
cy.

creed (krēd), n. **1** a brief statement of the main
points of religious belief of some church. **2** any
statement of faith, principles, opinions, etc.

cri ter i a (krī tir′ē ə), n. a pl. of **criterion.**

cri ter i on (krī tir′ē ən), n., pl. **-ter i a** or **-ter i ons.**
rule or standard for making a judgment; test:
Wealth is only one criterion of success.

cru cial (krü′shəl), adj. **1** very important or
decisive; critical. **2** very trying; severe. —
cru′cial ly, adv.

de bate (di bāt′), v., -bat ed, -bat ing. **1** discuss
reasons for and against; deliberate. **2** argue
about (a question, topic, etc.) in a public meeting. **3** think over in one's mind; consider: *I am
debating buying a camera.*

de lib e ra tion (di lib′ə rā′shən), n. **1** careful
thought: *After long deliberation, I decided not to
go.* **2** discussion of reasons for and against
something; debate: *the deliberations of Congress.* **3** slowness and care: *She drove the car
over the icy bridge with great deliberation.*

des o la tion (des′ə lā′shən), n. **1** act of making
desolate; devastation. **2** a ruined, lonely, or
deserted place. **3** a desolate place. **4** lonely
sorrow; sadness.

de tain (di tān′), v.t. **1** keep from going; hold back;
delay: *The heavy traffic detained us for almost
an hour.* **2** keep from going away; hold as a
prisoner: *The police detained the suspect for
further questioning.* **3** withhold.

dif fi cul ty (dif′ə kul′tē, dif′ə kəl tē), n., pl. **-ties.**
1 fact or condition of being difficult; degree to
which something is difficult: *The difficulty of the*

a hat	oi oil
ā age	ou out
ä far	u cup
e let	u̇ put
ē equal	ü rule
ėr term	
i it	ch child
ī ice	ng long
o hot	sh she
ō open	th thin
ô order	ŧʜ then
	zh measure

ə = {
  a in about
  e in taken
  i in pencil
  o in lemon
  u in circus
}

< = derived from

deliberation After much
deliberation, the boy
was ready to make his
move.

job prevented us from finishing it on time.
2 hard work; much effort: *I walked with difficulty after I sprained my ankle.* **3** something which stands in the way of getting things done; thing that is hard to do or understand. [< Latin *difficultatem* < *difficilis* hard < *dis-* + *facilis* easy]

dis cord (dis´kôrd), *n.* **1** disagreement of opinions and aims; dissension. **2** in music: **a** dissonance. **b** combination of two or more tones not in harmony with each other. **3** a clashing of sounds. **4** a harsh or unpleasing sound.

dis tin guished (dis ting´gwisht), *adj.* **1** famous; well-known: *a distinguished artist.* **2** looking important or superior.

dream (drēm), *n.* **1** images passing through the mind during sleep. **2** something as unreal as a dream. **3** condition in which a person has dreams. **4** something having great beauty or charm. **5** daydream; reverie.

expedition The **expedition** made camp at the base of the mountains.

e co nom ic (ē´kə nom´ik, ek´ə nom´ik), *adj.* **1** of or having to do with economics. Economic problems have to do with the production, distribution, and consumption of goods and services. **2** having to do with the management of the income, supplies, and expenses of a household, community, government, etc.

es sence (es´ns), *n.* that which makes a thing what it is; necessary part or parts; important feature or features: *Being thoughtful of others is the essence of politeness.*

ex pe di tion (ek´spə dish´ən), *n.* **1** journey for some special purpose, such as exploration, scientific study, or for military purposes. **2** the people, ships, etc., making such a journey.

ex tend (ek stend´), *v.t.* **1** stretch out: *extend your hand.* **2** continue or prolong in time, space, or direction: *I am extending my vacation another week.* **3** increase or enlarge: *They plan to extend their research in that field.*

fa nat ic (fə nat´ik), *n.* person who is carried away beyond reason because of feelings or beliefs, especially in religion or politics.

flat (flat), *n.* apartment.

flounce (flouns), *n.* a wide strip of cloth, gathered along the top edge and sewed to a dress, skirt, etc., for trimming; a wide ruffle.

fuse (fyüz), *n., v.,* **fused, fus ing.** —*n.* a slow-burning wick or other device used to set off a shell, bomb, a blast of gunpowder, or other explosive charge. —*v.t.* furnish with a fuse.

flounce The dancer's dress has a wide **flounce** on the bottom.

glance (glans), *n., v.,* **glanced, glanc ing.** —*n.* **1** a quick look directed at someone or something. **2** a flash of light; gleam. **3** a deflected motion; swift, slanting movement or impact. **4** a passing reference; brief allusion. —*v.i.* **1** look quickly: *glance at a page, glance out the window.*

hu mil i ty (hyü mil′ə tē), *n., pl.* **-ties.** humbleness of mind; meekness.

in flux (in′fluks), *n.* a flowing in; steady flow; inflow: *the influx of immigrants into a country.*

in sur rec tion (in′sə rek′shən), *n.* a rising against established authority; revolt; rebellion; uprising.

in tri guing (in trē′ging), *adj.* exciting the curiosity and interest: *an intriguing title.*

kin (kin), *n.* **1** a person's family or relatives; kindred. **2** family relationship; connection by birth or marriage: *What kin is she to you?*

lu cra tive (lü′krə tiv), *adj.* yielding gain or profit; profitable.

lu di crous (lu′də krəs), *adj.* causing derisive laughter; amusingly absurd; ridiculous.

me mo ri al (mə môr′ē əl, mə mōr′ē əl), *n.* **1** something that is a reminder of some event or person, such as a statue, an arch or column, a book, or a holiday. **2** statement sent to a government or person in authority, usually giving facts and asking that some wrong be corrected.

mer it (mer′it), *n.* **1** worth or value; goodness: *You will be marked according to the merit of your work.* **2** something that deserves praise or reward; commendable quality.

of fi cial (ə fish′əl), *n.* **1** person who holds a public position or who is in charge of some public work or duty: *The mayor is a government official.* **2** person holding office; officer: *bank officials.* —*adj.* **1** of or having to do with an office or officers: *an official uniform.* **2** having authority; authoritative: *An official record is kept of the proceedings of Congress.*

o ver come (ō′vər kum′), *v.t.,* **-came** (-kām′), **-come, -com ing. 1** get the better of; win the victory over; conquer; defeat: *overcome an enemy, overcome one's faults, overcome all difficulties.* **2** make weak or helpless: *overcome by weariness.*

memorial The Lincoln **Memorial** is in Washington, D.C.

pem mi can or **pem i can** (pem′ə kən), *n.* dried, lean meat pounded into a paste with melted fat and pressed into cakes. It was an important food among certain tribes of North American Indians.

per pet u al (pər pech′ü əl), *adj.* **1** lasting forever; eternal: *the perpetual hills.* **2** lasting throughout life: *a perpetual income.* **3** never ceasing; continuous; constant: *a perpetual stream of visitors.*

prom i nent (prom′ə nənt), *adj.* **1** well-known or important; distinguished: *a prominent citizen.* **2** that catches the eye; easy to see: *A single tree in a field is prominent.*

a	hat	oi	oil
ā	age	ou	out
ä	far	u	cup
e	let	ù	put
ē	equal	ü	rule
ėr	term		
i	it	ch	child
ī	ice	ng	long
o	hot	sh	she
ō	open	th	thin
ô	order	ŦH	then
		zh	measure

ə = { a in about
       e in taken
       i in pencil
       o in lemon
       u in circus

< = derived from

pueb lo (pweb′lō), *n., pl.* **-los. 1** an Indian village consisting of houses built of adobe and stone, usually with flat roofs and often several stories high. **2** in Spanish America, a village or town.

quill (kwil), *n.* **1** a large, stiff feather. **2** the hollow stem of a feather. **3** anything made from the hollow stem of a feather, such as a pen, toothpick, or an instrument for plucking the strings of a musical instrument. **4** the stiff, sharp, hollow spine of a porcupine or hedgehog —**quill-like,** *adj.*

quill work (kwil′wėrk), *n.* fabric, trimming, and other articles ornamented with or consisting of quills.

quo ta (kwō′tə), *n.* **1** the share or proportional part of a total due from or to a particular district, state, person, etc.: *Each member of the club was given a quota of tickets to sell for the party.* **2** a set number, amount, or portion: *I never exceed my quota of two cups of coffee a day.*

reb el (reb′əl), *n.* person who resists or fights against authority instead of obeying: *The rebels armed themselves against the government.*

res o lute (rez′ə lüt), *adj.* **1** having a fixed resolve; determined; firm. **2** constant in pursuing a purpose; bold. —**res′o lute′ly,** *adv.*

rev er ence (rev′ər əns), *n.* **1** a feeling of deep respect, mixed with wonder, awe, and love; veneration. **2** a deep bow. **3** condition of being greatly respected or venerated.

row dy (rou′dē), *n., pl.* **-dies,** *adj.,* **-di er, -di est.** —*n.* a rough, disorderly, quarrelsome person. —*adj.* rough; disorderly; quarrelsome.

rowdy The jester is a **rowdy** person.

ser e nade (ser′ə nād′), *n., v.,* **-nad ed, -nad ing.** —*n.* **1** music played or sung outdoors at night, especially by a lover under a sweetheart's window. **2** piece of music suitable for such a performance. —*v.t.* sing or play a serenade to. —*v.i.* sing or play a serenade.

sham ble (sham′bəl), *v.,* **-bled, -bling,** *n.* —*v.i.* walk awkwardly or unsteadily: *shamble across the room.* —*n.* a shambling walk.

site (sīt), *n.* position or place (of anything); location: *The site for the new school has not yet been chosen.*

suc cumb (sə kum′), *v.i.* **1** give way; yield: *succumb to temptation.* **2** die. —*v.t.* **succumb to,** die of.

sul len (sul′ən), *adj.* **1** silent because of bad humor or anger: *The sullen child refused to answer my question.* **2** showing bad humor or anger. **3** gloomy; dismal: *The sullen skies threatened rain.*

sullen The **sullen** child refused to look at me.

sur pass (sər pas′), *v.t.* **1** do better than; be greater than; excel: *Her work surpassed expectations.* **2** be too much or too great for; go beyond;

exceed: *The horrors of the battlefield surpassed description.*

swel ter ing (swel′tər ing), *adj.* extremely and unpleasantly hot. —**swel′ter ing ly,** *adv.*

sym pho ny (sim′fə nē), *n., pl.* **-nies. 1** an elaborate musical composition for an orchestra. It usually has three or more movements in different rhythms but related keys. **2** symphony orchestra. **3** concert by a symphony orchestra: *We're going to the symphony tonight.* **4** harmony of sounds. **5** harmony of colors: *Autumn leaves are a symphony in red, brown, and yellow.*

thresh old (thresh′ōld, thresh′hōld), *n.* **1** piece of wood or stone across the bottom of a door frame; doorsill. **2** doorway. **3** point of entering; beginning point: *The scientist was on the threshold of an important discovery.*

tim ber (tim′bər), *n.* **1** wood used for building, making furniture, etc. **2** a large piece of wood used in building, such as a beam or rafter. **3** a curved piece forming a rib of a ship. **4** growing trees; wooded land; forests. **5** trees bearing wood suitable for use in building.

trous seau (trü′sō, trü sō′), *n., pl.* **trous seaux** (trü′sōz, trü sōz′), **trous seaus.** a bride's outfit of clothes, linen, etc.

un chart ed (un chär′tid), *adj.* not mapped; not marked on a chart.

un der cov er (un′dər kuv′ər), *adj.* working or done in secret: *The jeweler was an undercover agent for the police.*

van ish (van′ish), *v.i.* **1** disappear, especially suddenly: *The sun vanished behind a cloud.*

vis u al ize (vizh′ü ə līz), *v.,* **-ized, -iz ing.** —*v.t.* **1** form a mental picture of: *visualize a friend's face when she is away.* **2** make visible.

vi tal (vī′tl), *adj.* **1** of or having to do with life: *Growth and decay are vital processes.* **2** necessary to life: *Eating is a vital function. The heart is a vital organ.* **3** very necessary; very important; essential: *a vital question. Drainage of the nearby swamp was considered vital to the welfare of the community.*

wear y (wir′ē), *adj.,* **wear i er, wear i est. 1** worn out; tired: *weary feet, a weary brain.* **2** causing tiredness; tiring: *a weary wait.* **3** having one's patience, tolerance, or liking exhausted: *be weary of excuses.* [Old English *wērig*] —**wear′i ly,** *adv.* —**wear′i ness,** *n.*

wist ful (wist′fəl), *adj.* longing; yearning: *A child stood looking with wistful eyes at the toys in the window.* —**wist′ful ly,** *adv.* —**wist′ful ness,** *n.*

a	hat	oi	oil
ā	age	ou	out
ä	far	u	cup
e	let	ù	put
ē	equal	ü	rule
ėr	term		
i	it	ch	child
ī	ice	ng	long
o	hot	sh	she
ō	open	th	thin
ô	order	ŦH	then
		zh	measure

ə = {
a in about
e in taken
i in pencil
o in lemon
u in circus

< = derived from

wistful Her **wistful** expression showed her sadness about moving.

Acknowledgments

Text

Page 7: From *Shades of Gray* by Carolyn Reeder. Copyright © 1989 by Carolyn Reeder. Reprinted with permission of Macmillan Publishing Company.

Page 22: "So I Became a Soldier" from *The Boys' War* by Jim Murphy. Text copyright © 1990 by Jim Murphy. Reprinted by permission of Clarion Books, a Houghton Mifflin Company imprint.

Page 32: Excerpt from *The Incredible Journey of Lewis and Clark* by Rhoda Blumberg. Copyright © 1987 by Rhoda Blumberg. Reprinted by permission of Lothrop, Lee & Shepard Books, a division of William Morrow & Company, Inc.

Page 43: From *Streams to the River, River to the Sea* by Scott O'Dell. Copyright © 1986 by Scott O'Dell. Reprinted by permission of Houghton Mifflin Company.

Page 65: "Railroads" from *An Illustrated History of the Chinese in America* by Ruthanne Lum McCunn. Copyright © 1979 by Ruthanne Lum McCunn. Reprinted by permission of Design Enterprises of San Francisco.

Page 70: "Spirits of the Railway" from *Tales from Gold Mountain: Stories of the Chinese in the New World* by Paul Yee. Text copyright © 1989 by Paul Yee. Reprinted with permission of Macmillan Publishing Company and Douglas & McIntyre Ltd., Canada.

Page 78: "Our Chinese Spirits" by Paul Yee. Copyright © by Paul Yee, 1991.

Page 83: Excerpted from *Crow and Weasel* by Barry Lopez. Copyright © 1990 by Barry Holstun Lopez; illustrations copyright © 1990 by Tom Pohrt. Published by North Point Press and reprinted by permission.

Page 92: From *American Women: Their Lives in Their Words* by Doreen Rappaport. Copyright © 1990 by Doreen Rappaport. Reprinted by permission of HarperCollins Publishers.

Page 101: "Being a Detective" by Doreen Rappaport. Copyright © by Doreen Rappaport, 1991.

Page 114: From *I Have a Dream* by Martin Luther King, Jr. Copyright © 1963 by Martin Luther King, Jr. Reprinted by permission of Joan Daves Agency.

Page 120: Excerpt from *The People, Yes* by Carl Sandburg. Copyright 1936 by Harcourt Brace Jovanovich, Inc. and renewed 1964 by Carl Sandburg. Reprinted by permission of the publisher.

Page 124: "The Vision of Maya Ying Lin" by Brent Ashabranner from *Always to Remember: The Story of the Vietnam Veterans Memorial*. Text copyright © 1988 by Brent Ashabranner. Photograph on page 130 copyright © 1988 by Jennifer Ashabranner. Reprinted by permission of G.P. Putnam's Sons.

Artists

Illustrations owned and copyrighted by the illustrator.
John Van Hammersveld: Cover, 1-5, 133-137
Kent Barton: 6-21
Dugald Stermer: 32-33
Michael Ward: 42-63
Ron Chan: 70-81
Tom Pohrt: 82, 89
Mary Lempa: 83-88, 90, 91
Carlos Cortez: 92-98

Seymour Chwast: 104-105
John Martinez: 120-121, 123
James Yang: 124-125

Photographs

Front Cover: Clockwise from top: Brown Brothers; Smithsonian Institution, National Anthropological Archives; Brown Brothers; Chicago Historical Society; Scheler/Black Star; Oregon Historical Society; Montana Historical Society

Back Cover: Top: Oregon Historical Society, cl: Myrleen Ferguson/PhotoEdit, cc: Freeman/Grishaber/PhotoEdit, cr: Mary Kate Denny/PhotoEdit, bl: Brent Jones, bc: Mary Kate Denny/PhotoEdit, br: David Young-Wolff/PhotoEdit

Page 1(tl), Mary Kate Denny/PhotoEdit; Page 1(tr), David Young-Wolff/PhotoEdit; Page 2(t), Tony Freeman/PhotoEdit; Page 2(cl), Brent Jones; Page 2(cr), New York Public Library; Page 2(br), Stephen McBrady/PhotoEdit

Page 3(tl), Freeman/Grishaber/PhotoEdit; Page 3(tr), Mary Kate Denny/PhotoEdit; Page 3(b), Brent Jones

Page 4(bl), Bill Aron/PhotoEdit; Page 4(br), Tony Freeman/PhotoEdit

Page 5(tl), Keystone Mast Collection, California Museum of Photography, University of California at Riverside; Page 5(tr), David Young-Wolff/PhotoEdit

Page 22 (top to bottom): Library of Congress, Chicago Historical Society, Library of Congress, Chicago Historical Society

Page 23 (first row, top to bottom): Collection of Mr. William S. Powell, Chapel Hill, NC; Library of Congress; Chicago Historical Society; Library of Congress

Page 23 (second row, top to bottom): Library of Congress, Chicago Historical Society, Library of Congress, Chicago Historical Society

Page 23 (third row, top to bottom): Chicago Historical Society, Library of Congress, Chicago Historical Society, Library of Congress

Pages 25, 27, 69, 116–117: Library of Congress

Page 28: Chicago Historical Society

Page 31: Courtesy of the collection of Tim McCarthy

Page 41: Missouri Historical Society

Pages 64–65: Special Collections Division, University of Washington Libraries

Page 67: Western History Collection, Denver Public Library

Page 78: Courtesy of Paul Yee

Page 100: Courtesy of Doreen Rappaport

Page 100: Steve Greiner

Page 106: Brown Brothers

Pages 109, 111: The Museum of the City of New York

Pages 114–115: Scheler/Black Star

Page 119: Don Uhrbrock/Life Magazine Time Warner Inc.

Page 129: Richard Howard/Black Star

Page 130: Jennifer Ashabranner from *Always to Remember* by Brent Ashabranner

Glossary

The contents of the Glossary entries in this book have been adapted from Scott Foresman *Advanced Dictionary*, copyright © 1988 by Scott, Foresman and Company.

Page 140 (top): Stuart Cohen/Stock Boston; Page 140 (bottom): Tom Myers; Page 141: Vance Henry; Page 142 (top): From the collection of Carol Hatcher

Unless otherwise acknowledged, all photographs are the property of ScottForesman.